Six Sigma^{+Lean} Toolset

Stephan Lunau (Ed.)

Alexander John
Renata Meran
Olin Roenpage
Christian Staudter

Six Sigma$^{+\text{Lean}}$ Toolset

Executing Improvement Projects Successfully

Translated by Astrid Schmitz

 Springer

Editor:
Dipl.-Kfm. Stephan Lunau
UMS GmbH Consulting
Hanauer Landstraße 291B
60314 Frankfurt
Germany
sl@ums-gmbh.com

Authors:
Dr.-Ing. Alexander John
Dipl.-Vw. Renata Meran
Mag. Olin Roenpage
Dipl.-Bw. Christian Staudter

UMS GmbH Consulting
Hanauer Landstraße 291B
60314 Frankfurt
Germany

ISBN 978-3-540-32349-5   e-ISBN 978-3-540-32350-1

Library of Congress Control Number: 2008935026

© 2008 Springer-Verlag Berlin Heidelberg

This work is subject to copyright. All rights are reserved, whether the whole or part of the material is concerned, specifically the rights of translation, reprinting, reuse of illustrations, recitation, broadcasting, reproduction on microfilm or in any other way, and storage in data banks. Duplication of this publication or parts thereof is permitted only under the provisions of the German Copyright Law of September 9, 1965, in its current version, and permissions for use must always be obtained from Springer-Verlag. Violations are liable for prosecution under the German Copyright Law.

The use of general descriptive names, registered names, trademarks, etc. in this publication does not imply, even in the absence of a specific statement, that such names are exempt from the relevant protective laws and regulations and therefore free for general use.

Cover design: WMXDesign GmbH, Heidelberg, Germany

Printed on acid-free paper

9 8 7 6 5 4 3 2 1

springer.com

Table of Contents

Contents

Contents

Foreword

Six Sigma has established itself globally over the last 20 years as a best practice concept for optimizing processes. Many renowned companies from a diverse array of business branches successfully deploy Six Sigma and profit from the benefits of Six Sigma-inspired projects, significantly improving their net income. Focusing on customer needs and measurability is at the forefront of this approach.

In the course of its long history the Six Sigma approach has undergone many developments and upgrades and these have been incorporated into the original concept. One very important step is the integration of Lean Management tools into the classical Six Sigma concept. Along with reducing process variation – which is achieved through classical quality tools and statistical analysis, these tools contribute decisively to achieving a significant acceleration in process speed and a reduction of inventories and lead times.

As practiced by UMS GmbH, in its applications, the Six Sigma^{+Lean} approach thus combines the tried-and-tested tools of both worlds, which are linked together systematically in the proven DMAIC process model. Effective tools exist for every problem, ensuring that excellent and sustainable project results are achieved.

We took the chance to update the book with respect to the latest developments of the method and incorporated the customer feedback of the last years.

Here we focused especially on an improved Define phase, the incorporation of the OEE measurement in the Measure phase and a revised Lean Toolset.

The present Six Sigma^{+Lean} Toolset takes into account the described developments by serving as a practice-oriented reference book for trained Master Black Belts, Black Belts, and Green Belts. It contains all key Six Sigma^{+Lean} tools, which are depicted in clearly structured graphs, charts and highlighted with examples. The book follows the successive phases of a project and deals with the tools according to their respective place in the Define, Measure, Analyze, Improve, and Control phases. This enables the expert to work through his projects chronologically, with the Toolset acting as a guideline.

I am indebted to members of the UMS team; their detailed expertise and rich wealth of experience contributed to realizing this Toolset. In particular my co-authors Alexander John, Renata Meran, Olin Roenpage, and Christian Staudter. I would like to thank Astrid Schmitz for her effort in the translation and adaptation process. Finally, my thanks go to Mariana Winterhager for her continuous effort in incorporating all the changes and the improvements into the Toolset.

I wish readers good luck with their projects.
Frankfurt am Main, July 2008
Stephan Lunau

Six Sigma^{+Lean}
Toolset

Introduction

Introduction

Contents:

The Formula for Success
- The core elements for a successful implementation of Six Sigma^{+Lean}

Quality as Success Factor
- The foundations and dimensions of Six Sigma^{+Lean}
- What is Six Sigma^{+Lean}?
- Six Sigma^{+Lean} puts benefit first
- What does the term Six Sigma^{+Lean} mean?
- The dimensions of project success in Six Sigma^{+Lean}
- Improving processes (DMAIC)
- Developing new processes or products (DFSS)

Acceptance as Success Factor
- Roles and responsibilities in the Six Sigma^{+Lean} concept
- Modular and practice-oriented training and coaching concept

Management Commitment as Success Factor
- On the road to business excellence
- Implementation concepts
- Methodological Six Sigma^{+Lean} generations

Result: Measurable, Sustainable Success
- What is "Critical to Quality" when implementing Six Sigma^{+Lean}?

The Formula for Success: Core Elements of Successful Six Sigma^{+Lean} Implementation

The Success Formula for Six Sigma^{+Lean} Implementation

For over nine years now, UMS has implemented Six Sigma^{+Lean} in a diverse array of corporate structures and cultures. The experience we have gained shows that certain core elements are crucial for achieving measurable and sustainable results. These core elements can be defined as success factors and presented in the following compact formula:

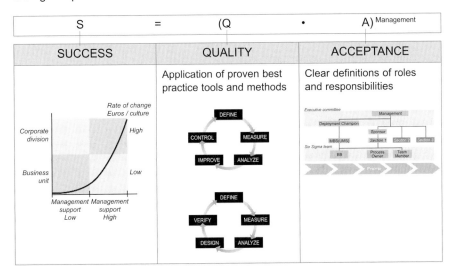

Quality describes the consistent and sensible application of proven best practice tools and methods for optimizing existing processes and developing new processes and products. The sum of this work on processes and products is an important contribution to achieving process excellence in the corporation – methodologically advanced and supported by the Six Sigma^{+Lean} concept.

The application of the methods takes place in the framework of clearly defined roles and responsibilities for employees and managers in the corporation. In the course of this application, an extensive knowledge of methods is built up amongst employees in a short time. This knowledge creates an independence from external support when faced with solving upcoming problems. In turn, this employee competence decides primarily about the **acceptance** of the concept in the corporation and influences significantly the implementation. Dedicated resources which are given the relevant freedom to do their project work in the framework of Six Sigma^{+Lean} deliver quick and measurable results.

Intensive training in methods for employees in combination with practical project work generates both a direct transfer of knowledge as well as benefits and palpable progress for one's own projects. The combined training and coaching in the frame of the Six Sigma^{+Lean} project work positively influences project culture, provides adequate support through all project phases, and thus represents a key element for achieving people excellence.

How can quality and acceptance be secured and strengthened when implementing Six Sigma^{+Lean}? With adequate **management** commitment clear and measurable goals, connected to the current corporate strategy, focus existing resources on the important themes. These are to be defined through a value-based project selection. Here, top management takes on a key role model function. On the one hand, the goals to be achieved with Six Sigma^{+Lean} in project works are to be integrated into existing incentive structures, on the other, the aspiration must be to achieve the trans-sectoral application of the concept in the sense of a common language to change corporate culture.

In their overall effect, the listed elements of the success formula result in a quick, measurable **success** that, along with a noticeable generation of net benefit, also achieves a considerable contribution to business excellence in the sum of the selected success factors.

The following section will present and explain the individual core elements of the formula:

Success = (Quality • Acceptance)^{Management}.

***Quality as Success Factor: The Foundations and Dimensions of
Six Sigma^{+Lean}***

What is Six Sigma^{+Lean}?

Six Sigma^{+Lean} is the consistent further development and systematic interlinking of proven tools and methods. When combined coherently and applied consistently, they can also be considered and employed as an integrated approach for changing corporate culture.

The following table visualizes the differences to other approaches and methods:

Six Sigma^{+Lean}	**=**	**the creation of lean processes free of variation as well as customer-oriented products.**
Product development	=	develop processes and products.
Lean management	=	cut process cost.
TQM	=	optimize / manage processes.
ISO	=	standardize / optimize processes.

Six Sigma⁺ᴸᵉᵃⁿ *Puts Benefit First*

Six Sigma⁺ᴸᵉᵃⁿ shows that a demand for raising quality while simultaneously reducing costs must not be a contradiction. Instead, the task set in every project is to consider and realize both sides of the "Six Sigma" coin.

Raising quality and customer satisfaction

Project benefit for the company in €

Because only misunderstood quality costs money: putting quality into the product independent of customer requirements generates higher costs, and these can add up to a significant share of turnover. For example, with a three Sigma process poor quality accounts for up to 30 % of turnover (cost of poor quality), a factor that is also known as the "hidden factory". If quality is understood correctly, then it generates financial gain: because quality is what the customer is willing to pay for. For the customer this means that perceivable quality is produced through lean processes at significantly lower costs.

From this key consideration we can derive the special vision of quality that is the hallmark of Six Sigma⁺ᴸᵉᵃⁿ and always puts benefit first:
The requirements of our customers are to be met completely and profitably.

Waste frequently represents the largest cost driver (called the "hidden factory" in industrial corporations). Starting points for optimization are to be found in the following areas:
- Rework
- Duplication of work
- Rejects / defects
- Inventories and warehousing

Hidden factory (ca. 30 %)

Here a cost reduction of up to 30 % can be generated. In addition, increasing qual-
ity creates the preconditions necessary for raising turnover. Overall, the following
levers emerge for net benefit:
- Increasing quality – customer loyalty and realizing greater turnover levels
- Cost reductions – greater competitive potential
- Higher process speed – less stock
- Greater customer loyalty – realization of new business fields

What Does the Term Six Sigma[+Lean] Mean?

Six Sigma[+Lean] means "six standard deviations". The Six Sigma[+Lean] vision means
that the standard deviation of a normal distribution fits +/- six times between the
specification limits defined by the customer (upper specification limit = USL and
lower specification limit = LSL). The located value corresponds to a quality level
of 99.9999998 %. Practical experience shows that processes fluctuate over time
– by at least +/-1.5 Sigma, this means that in the end a quality level of 99.9997 %
is achieved and this corresponds to an error rate of 3.4 defects per million opportunities (DPMO).

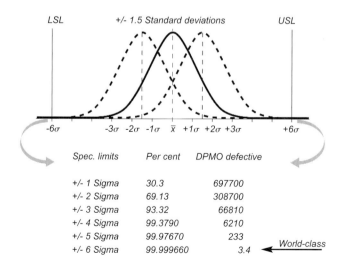

Spec. limits	Per cent	DPMO defective
+/- 1 Sigma	30.3	697700
+/- 2 Sigma	69.13	308700
+/- 3 Sigma	93.32	66810
+/- 4 Sigma	99.3790	6210
+/- 5 Sigma	99.97670	233
+/- 6 Sigma	99.999660	3.4

World-class ←

Six Sigma^{+Lean} stands for a customer-driven maximization of quality that provides measurability and a data-driven procedure based on a statistically secured ana- lytic ("whatever cannot be measured cannot be improved"). Numbers, data, and facts accompany every project and support both the description of the current situ- ation as well as the systematic analysis of causes.

The Dimensions of Project Success in Six Sigma^{+Lean}

Six Sigma^{+Lean} is made up of four important modules or dimensions that secure project success
- The iterative cycle employed to optimize processes, called the DMAIC, that is made up of the five phases, **D**efine, **M**easure, **A**nalyze, **I**mprove, and **C**ontrol
- The procedural model for developing processes and products, called the DMADV that is made up of the five phases, **D**efine, **M**easure, **A**nalyze, **D**esign, and **V**erifiy – (also known as DFSS, Design for Six Sigma^{+Lean})
- Lean tools applied in the two aforementioned approaches
- Process management for securing sustainability

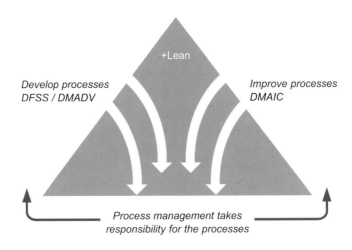

Improving Processes (DMAIC)

The DMAIC iterative cycle employed to optimize existing processes forms the basis for systematic and fact-based project work that achieves sustainable and measurable results. The aim of DMAIC is to raise quality (by reducing rework and scrap) and reduce stocks as well as cutting cycle times through inventory controls and adjusting capacity.

When applying the DMAIC cycle, the following mindset is used to solve the identified, complex problems:

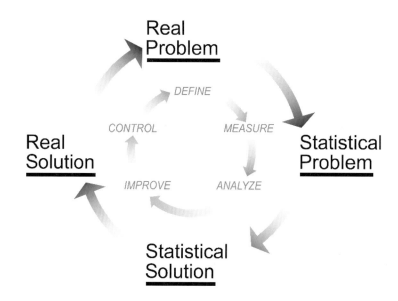

The following chart lists the main activities and aligns the tools employed to the respective phase:

	Tools	Mission
Define	• Project Charter • SIPOC • CTQ Matrix • Stakeholder Analysis	• The project is defined. • Current state and target state are depicted and the process to be improved is marked off. • Customer and business requirements are clearly defined.
Measure	• Measurement Matrix • Operational Definition • Measurement System Analysis • Sample Size and Strategy • Charts and Diagrams • Quality Key Figures	• The starting situation is captured. • Key figures and an operational definition are developed, the measurement system analysis is completed, and the data collected.
Analyze	• Cause & Effect Diagram • FMEA • Process Analysis • Value Stream Map • Hypothesis Tests • Regression • DOE	• The causes for the problem are identified. • All possible causes are collected and summarized into the decisive key figures through process and data analysis.
Improve	• Brainstorming • "Must" Criteria • Effort-Benefit Matrix • Criteria-based Selection • Piloting • Roll out Planning	• The solution is implemented. • Possible solutions are generated on the basis of core causes, systematically selected, and prepared for implementation.
Control	• Documentation • Procedural Instructions • Control and Run Charts • Reaction Plan and Process Management Diagrams	• The sustainability of the result is secured. • The implemented solutions are documented and will be monitored using key figures. • A reaction plan secures prompt intervention.

Special tools and methods taken from lean management have complemented and extended the DMAIC toolbox over the last few years – the result is the Six Sigma[+Lean] concept. This development was undertaken on the basis of an important insight: that, along with reducing process variation through proven quality tools and statistical analyses, the relevant levers for achieving significant cuts in cycle time and inventories are also of great importance. This fundamental prevention or avoidance of waste will be a continuous focus of our considerations.

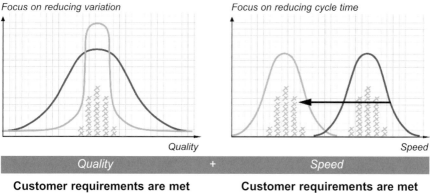

Focus on reducing variation	Focus on reducing cycle time
Quality	*Speed*

Quality	+	Speed
Customer requirements are met completely		**Customer requirements are met profitably**
Tools of quality management		Tools of lean management

The following lean tools have proven worthwhile and are integrated into the DMAIC iterative cycle:

	Lean tools	*Mission*
Analyze	• Value Stream Map • Identification of the Sources of Waste • Little's Law • Process Efficiency • Constraints Analysis (takt rates and takt time analysis)	• The root causes are identified. • The causes for constraints, high stock inventories and long cycle times are identified and summarized into root causes by using lean tools.
Improve	• Theory of Constraints (TOC) • 5 S • Setup Time Reduction • Generic Pull System • Replenishment Pull System • Poka Yoke • Total Productive Maintenance (TPM) • Lean for Service	• The solutions are implemented. • Based on the core causes and using lean tools the solutions are developed, evaluated, and prepared for implementation.

Exemplary depiction of relevant project topics in the frame of Six Sigma[+Lean]:

Quality-related topics *= variation reduction*	*Speed-related topics* *= increasing process speed*
• Reducing rework / scrap • Optimizing quality reviews • Optimizing output (less waste) • Reducing customer complaints • Systematic optimization of machinery parameters through Design of Experiments (DOE) • Reducing complexity: one component serves several applications	• Significant inventory reduction • Minimize trans-sectoral cycle times, e.g. reduce order to cash • Improve process efficiency by reducing waste • Raise capacity by balancing out processes and improving availability of machines • Optimize setup times to reduce batch sizes and the necessary inventories

The DMAIC methodology helps to effectively reduce or even eliminate the so-called negative quality. Negative quality arises when defined customer requirements are not met profitably.

The DMADV procedural model for process and product development generates positive quality in the sense of a strongly customer- and market-oriented development of products and processes. In this way, DMADV maximizes potential by generating value for the customer.

"Not doing anything wrong does not mean you're doing everything right!"

DMAIC	DMADV / DFSS
Eliminating negative quality	Generating positive quality
• Quality / reduce defects • Speed / increase speed • Costs / reduce costs	• Problem solving • Creating opportunities • Look good • Feel good

Project work with the DMADV model focuses on the effort to offer customers products and processes, which have value for them, i.e. to recognize, understand, and implement customer needs. Innovative work on the new or further development of products and of processes is pressed ahead with by taking into account the prerequisite for solving problems from a customer viewpoint, for demonstrating new opportunities, and for feeling good, and / or looking good.

Developing New Processes or Products (DFSS)

In DFSS value for the customer is created by using the DMADV methodology and recognizing the relevant value drivers:

1. **Problem solving:** Helps the customer to **solve** an existing **problem**	2. **Creating opportunities:** Helps the customer to create new **opportunities** that do not yet exist
4. **Feel good:** Helps the customer to **feel good** about themselves	3. **Look good:** Helps the customer to **look good** in comparison to competitors

Product / Process — Value, Value, Value, Value

The prerequisite for this is a systematic elaboration of "true" customer needs and their prioritization. The aim of developmental work is not the development of a product based on the latest technology (running the risk of "over engineering"), but rather the best possible implementation of customer needs in solutions that create products and processes with value for the customer.

The following table lists the main tasks and aligns the tools to the respective DMADV phase.

	Tools	Mission
Define	• Project Charter • Project Scope • Multigeneration Plan (MGP) • Gantt Chart • RACI Chart • Budget Calculation • Stakeholder Analysis Table • Communication Plan • Risk Analysis	• The project is defined. • Problem and goal are defined and complimented by a Multigeneration Plan. • The project is clearly marked off and the influence on other projects examined. • The activity, time, and resources planning are defined. Possible project risks assessed.
Measure	• Portfolio Analysis • Kano Model • Customer Interaction Study • Survey Techniques • Affinity Diagram • Tree Diagram • Benchmarking • House of Quality • Design Scorecard	• The relevant customers are identified and segmented. • Customer needs are collected, sorted, and prioritized. • CTQs and measurements are deduced on the basis of customer needs. • Priorities are set for measurements and the target values, specifications, and quality key figures are defined.
Analyze	• Function Analysis • Transfer Function • Creativity Techniques • Ishikawa Diagram • TRIZ • Benchmarking • Pugh Matrix • FMEA • Anticipated Error Detection • Design Scorecard • Process Modeling • Prototyping	• The best concept is selected from the alternative high-level concepts. • Conflicts and contradictions in the selected concept are resolved and the requirements to the necessary resources are derived. • The remaining risk is defined, customer feedback was obtained, and the concept finalized.
Design	• Statistical Procedures (tolerancing, hypothesis tests, DOE) • Design Scorecard • FMEA • Radar Chart • Lean Toolbox (Value Stream Design, Pull Systems, SMED / Quick Changeover, Lot Sizing, Complexity, Poka Yoke, Process Balancing)	• The detailed design is developed, optimized, and evaluated. • The production process is planned and optimized based on lean specifications. • The implementation of the process design is prepared, involved employees are informed, and customer feedback was obtained.

Tools	Mission
Verify • PDCA Cycle • Project Management • Training • SOPs • KDI Monitoring	• The pilot is carried out, analyzed, and the roll out planned. • The production process is implemented. • The process is completely handed over to the process owner, the documentation was handed over, and the project concluded.

This Toolset doesn't take into account the DFSS concept. DFSS is covered by the DFSS[+Lean] Toolset we published in 2007.

Acceptance as Success Factor

Roles and Responsibilities in the Six Sigma^{+Lean} Concept

The key aspects that need to be put into place for a universal acceptance of Six Sigma[+Lean] are clearly defined roles and responsibilities for employees and executives, intensive method training, and coaching accompanying the improvement projects.

Along with a corporate-specific customization and definition of the roles, their systematic implementation in everyday practice is an important task and challenge in Six Sigma[+Lean] deployments.

The chart below shows the typical roles (followed by a detailed description).

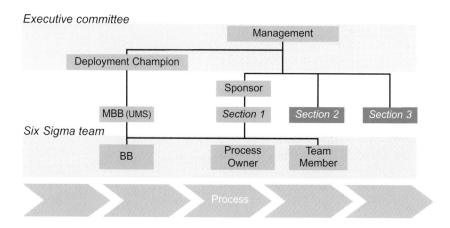

Executive committee
- Defines the strategic orientation of Six Sigma[+Lean]
- Prioritizes and decides on the projects and sets the project mission
- Chooses the Project Sponsor for each project
- Carries out regular reviews

Deployment Champion
- Steers and drives forward the Six Sigma^{+Lean} initiative
- Defines unified standards used in Six Sigma^{+Lean}
- Guides and instructs the Master Black Belts
- Ensures the support of top management
- Identifies and shows the benefits of Six Sigma^{+Lean}

Project Sponsor (also called the Champion in some organizations)
- Guarantees that the required resources are available and assembles the project team
- Is responsible for the project's monetary results
- Reports to the executive committee
- Carries out regular gate reviews (sign offs) together with the Black Belt and Master Black Belt

Master Black Belt (MBB)
- Is engaged full-time in the Six Sigma^{+Lean} initiative and coaches the Black Belts and Green Belts
- Carries out the regular gate reviews for the project phases
- Coordinates projects and project proposals
- Identifies training needs and carries out further training measures
- Is assigned to specific core processes (and Process Owners)

Black Belt (BB)
- Is engaged full-time in the Six Sigma^{+Lean} initiative
- Guides the Six Sigma^{+Lean} projects, contributes his / her methodological competence, and leads the team to success
- Is responsible for both the management of the project as well as its documentation
- Regularly informs the Project Sponsor and organizes the gate reviews
- Along with direct involvement in project work performs other tasks in the scope of the Six Sigma^{+Lean} initiative (work packages)

Green Belt (GB)
- Is engaged part-time in the Six Sigma^{+Lean} initiative
- Guides smaller Six Sigma^{+Lean} improvement projects in his / her section or supports a Black Belt, contributes his / her methodological competence, and leads the team to success
- Is responsible for project management and its documentation together with a Black Belt
- Regularly informs the Project Sponsor

Team Member (Yellow Belt)
- Works constructively both within and outside the team meetings on the work packages and contributes his / her professional competence
- Supports the implementation of the project and acts as a multiplier of the initiative

Process Owner
- Implements the results generated by the improvement project
- Ensures the long-term sustainability of the project results
- Communicates early on and regularly with the Black Belt and Sponsor

Along with the deployment of DMAIC / DMADV tools and methods and the accompanying support of project work with the aid of defined roles, reporting progress is crucial for monitoring and presenting achieved results. The graph below is an excellent example of a reporting structure and is typical of a Six Sigma^{+Lean} organization. This kind of structure supports the translation of the defined roles into actual work and so guarantees its successful completion.

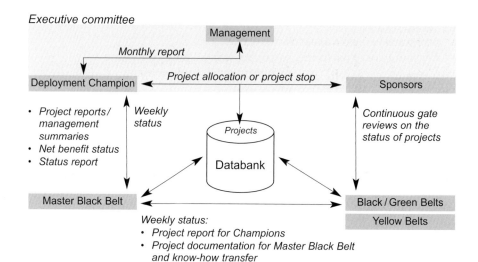

20

A Modular and Practice-oriented Training and Coaching Concept

A modular-based training and coaching of Black and Green Belts guarantees that project work remains practically relevant, if it is combined with continuous references to the specific improvement projects between the modules. The Master Black Belts act as direct coaches for the Black and Green Belts. In this way they ensure an intensive knowledge transfer of the Six Sigma^{+Lean} methodology and its tools from the training into their own project work and that their application is suitable for dealing with specific problems and tasks.

For this reason, tools and methods are taught in concentrated form and can be applied to the projects in flexible combinations. When structured in this way, the Master Black Belt is the key contact partner for training and coaching – this secures maximum effectiveness for the whole course of the project.

Group coaching sessions – where several participants come together to discuss the project – can further intensify know-how transfer because they provide insights into comprehensive problems and how they may be approached.

Combined method training for Six Sigma^{+Lean} Black Belts:

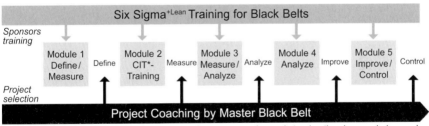

*CIT = Change implementation tools, a concept for accompanying and steering the changes being made to a process

Combined method training for Six Sigma^{+Lean} Green Belts:

Each of the modules is characterized by a didactic "triple jump". The first stage is the teaching of theoretical content. In the second stage this theory is applied to simulations and exercises, modeled on actual business cases enabling participants to practice transferring their knowledge to practically relevant situations. The third stage is devoted to working on one's own projects, guaranteeing that knowledge is transferred directly to specific problems in project work.

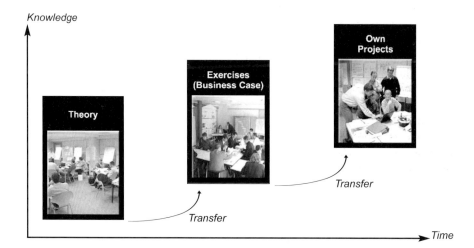

This approach allows training to be conducted flexibly, responsive to the specific requirements and needs of the participants. Project-related problems can be integrated into the training and coaching at all times. Controls are carried out at the completion to monitor learning success; they provide both the participants as well as the responsible Master Black Belt with feedback on the strengths and weaknesses of each participant.

Management Commitment as Success Factor

On the Road to Business Excellence

A consistent management support is the key to success – irrespective of the scope of Six Sigma[+Lean] in the organization at its launch.

Six Sigma[+Lean] unfolds its full effect when the concept's core elements are applied across and permeate through the entire organization – such a complete and systematic approach is the motor of success.

Six Sigma[+Lean] is ideally suited to support a corporation on the road to achieving business excellence. Process excellence is created along with the application of proven tools. Employees are integrated and empowered in the sense of people excellence. The greatest benefit of Six Sigma[+Lean] lies in the creation of a conceptual, fact-based framework that enables performance to be measured, improved, and managed. This generates in turn the transparency necessary for management to make the right decisions. In this way Six Sigma[+Lean] actively supports the implementation of corporate strategy.

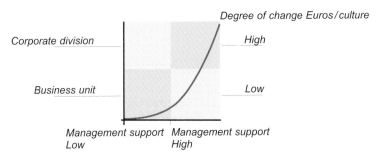

Degree of change Euros/culture

Corporate division   *High*

Business unit   *Low*

Management support   *Management support*
Low   *High*

Consistent management support means measurable monetary results which as a rule already surpass the cumulative expenses in the first year of the Six Sigma[+Lean] application. Practice shows that a consistent application of the Six Sigma[+Lean] concept can lead to a cost/effort-benefit ratio of 1:7 and more.

"Do it right the first time" describes the general aspiration of business excellence – but it especially covers the **methodological** and **scheduled development phases** of a Six Sigma[+Lean] implementation.

Implementation Approaches

In terms of timing, progress when implementing Six Sigma[+Lean] can be achieved either through a step-by-step approach or in one quick step, known as a break-through approach. Both approaches have their own strengths and weaknesses.

Step by step:
- Phased build up of Six Sigma[+Lean] resources
- Lower net benefits at the start of the initiative
- The implementation is manageable and controllable
- Continuous build up of knowledge and permanent refining of expertise
- Continuous change of corporate culture
- Acceptance of the Six Sigma[+Lean] program is generated and extended continually

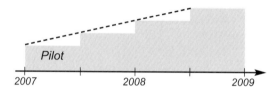

Break through:
- Training for numerous Six Sigma[+Lean] resources at the very start of the initiative
- Quicker generation of benefit in the projects at the start of the implementation
- Considerable cost and effort required to manage and coordinate
- High risk of identifying and implementing the wrong resources and projects
- Danger of increasing resistance due to the excessive demands made on the organization by carrying out numerous projects in the implementation phase
- A rapid change of culture in the corporation is necessary

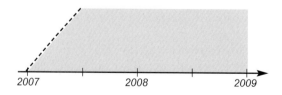

Methodical Creation of Six Sigma^{+Lean} Generations

A methodical development means orientating the projects on the selected methodological approach of DMAIC and/or DMADV. One tried and tested strategy is to first take a purely internal perspective and focus on optimizing processes that include internal customers. In most cases, carrying out projects on the basis of this strategy is based on the premise that existing potential can be turned into reality by eliminating defects. This has the added benefit of providing the persons involved with suitable practice in using tools and methods.

Over time and with greater experience the project focus changes to external customers. This approach shall be increasingly externalized in a further developed generation, i.e. it becomes increasingly geared towards customers and markets so as to place "valuable" products or processes of a positive quality (Phase 3).

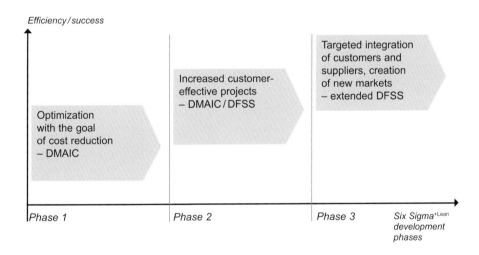

Efficiency/success

Optimization with the goal of cost reduction – DMAIC

Increased customer-effective projects – DMAIC/DFSS

Targeted integration of customers and suppliers, creation of new markets – extended DFSS

Phase 1   *Phase 2*   *Phase 3*   *Six Sigma^{+Lean} development phases*

25

Result: Measurable, Sustainable Success

What is "Critical to Quality" in a Six Sigma^{+Lean} Implementation?

In summary, the following factors are critical for achieving success in a Six Sigma^{+Lean} implementation:

$$(\text{Quality} \cdot \text{Acceptance})^{\text{Management}} = \text{Success}$$

	Quality	Acceptance	Management	Success
A strong Deployment Champion	X	X	X	X
Consequent management commitment		X	X	X
Consistent project selection in Sponsor trainings		X	X	X
Key figure driven project selection	X	X	X	X
Early integration of works council		X		X
Information events for employees (2-3 hours)		X		X
Available methodological experts (Master Black Belt)	X	X		X
Continuous gate reviews with Sponsor and team	X	X	X	X
Available documents and materials – Net benefit guidelines – Project workbooks etc.	X	X		X
Universally applied methods and shared language	X	X		X
Availability of Six Sigma^{+Lean} resources		X	X	X

Six Sigma^{+Lean}
Toolset

DEFINE

Phase 1: Define

Goals

- Describe the specific problem, identify the project's goal and exact scope.
- Determine the key customers of the process to be optimized as well as their CTQs.
- Ensure that the project gains acceptance.

Steps

- Review and agree on the project charter. Carry out project kick-off meeting.
- Depict the process for optimization on a high level and within the scope of the defined focus.
- Identify the important external / internal customers of the process.
- Translate customer voices into measurable CTQs.
- Identify stakeholders and opinion makers and integrate them to ensure project success.

Key Tools

- **Project Charter**

- **SIPOC**

- **Customer Orientation**

- **Research Methods for Collecting Customer Needs**

- **Customer Voice Chart**

- **Kano Model**

- **Tool 1: CTQ Matrix / CTB Matrix**

- **Stakeholder Analysis**

- **Kick-Off Meeting**

- **Gate Review**

DEFINE

Project Charter

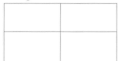

Kick-Off Meeting

SIPOC Process Diagram

S	I	P	O	C

Tool 1: CTQ Matrix

Complaint	Solution	Specification	Other	"True" need	CTQs

Stakeholder Analysis

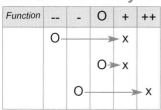

Function	--	-	O	+	++
		O——→ x			
			O→x		
		O———→ x			

Gate Review

MEASURE

ANALYZE

IMPROVE

CONTROL

DEFINE

MEASURE

ANALYZE

IMPROVE

CONTROL

Project Charter

🗂 Terms
Project charter, team charter, project order, project sheet

🕐 When
Prior to the first meeting with the project team (kick-off meeting)

◎ Goals
- Depict the problems and project goals briefly and clearly.
- Focus clearly on a specific process or sub-process for optimization.
- Nominate all the important project participants.

▸▸ Steps
- The Sponsor draws up the project charter in collaboration with the Black Belt.
- Hold background talks to clarify the contents covered by the project charter with direct and indirect participants at an early stage.
  The project charter contains the following elements:

1. Business Case
Describe the starting situation and emphasize what the project means and its importance.

2. Problems and Goals
Describe problems and goals the SMART way (Specific, Measurable, Agreed to, Realistic, Time bound). Do not guess causes or propose solutions, but depict the current and target state. Besides the baseline (the basis for savings achieved by the project and the additional turn-over), estimate the monetary benefits of the project (net benefit).

3. Focus and Scope
Which issues are within and which are outside the project scope?
What is to be the focus?
For the DMAIC approach, which process forms the basis?

Project Charter

DEFINE

MEASURE

ANALYZE

IMPROVE

CONTROL

4. Roles and Milestones

Fix the starting date of the project and its duration (max. 90 days, for exceptions up to 180 days), name the involved persons, and determine the resources needed.

A separate project schedule for the whole project is required. Further possible components of the project charter are:

- Key quality indicators (e.g. current Sigma value, DPMO).
- Improvements or project benefits which cannot be calculated in metrics.
- Risks that may impede carrying out the project or realizing the full benefit.

⇨ Tips

- State the "compelling need" for the project in the business case.
- Consider the SMART rule. The launch of many projects fail due to abstract and imprecise descriptions of problems and goals.
- Consult alternative experts as part of an extended team. There should be no more than five team members "on board" so as to conserve resources.
- Discuss the key facets of the project charter with the team members before the kick-off meeting.
- After the formulation of the final definition, the Sponsor at the very least, signs the project charter.
- The project charter is a living document: New insights, in particular data and monetary calculations, are to be integrated into the project charter. The project charter is realigned after the completion of each phase.
- The project charter is the project's calling card: The most important information pertaining to the project can be listed clearly and compactly on a single page.

DEFINE

MEASURE

ANALYZE

IMPROVE

CONTROL

Example of a Project Charter
Example: car dealer

Business Case

We are a car dealer selling many different brands and providing repair services. We employ 80 persons at our main operations as well as 20 at each of our two branches. With competition becoming fiercer and the market situation increasingly difficult, it is proving nearly impossible to operate profitably purely through sales. It is therefore important that we focus on earning profits from our repair services, panel-beating and spray-painting operations, and the sale of parts and accessories. Turnover in our panel-beating and spray-operating division has dipped over the last two years.
Besides the number of customers complaining about the quality of the spray-painting has increased. The running costs here are no longer in line with the market.
A Six Sigma^{+Lean} DMAIC project is established to make this division successful again.

Project Scope/Project Focus

In:
The process flow from accepting the job, preparing and applying the paint and final paint, to the final control of the vehicle

Out:
Personnel costs, warranty and callbacks by the manufacturer

Problems and Goals

Problem (current state)
30 % of spray-painting jobs have to be redone due to customer complaints.
In 2005, rework caused additional costs of € 63,000 and a 20 % slump in turnover (to € 384,000).

Goal (target state)
Rework reduction to a maximum of 5 % in the coming year. Turnover to be increased to € 560,000.

Roles and Milestones

Team:	Define:	1/23/06
Mr. Stolle (15 man days)	Measure:	2/06/06
Mr. Rimac (3 man days)	Analyze:	2/27/06
Mr. Calabrese (15 man days)	Improve:	3/20/06
Mr. Engers (3 man days)	Control:	4/18/06

Sponsor:
Head of customer services, Mr. Vetter

Black Belt:
Paint workshop supervisor, Mr. Goldbach (3 man days)

Process Owner:
Mr. Vetter

Timeframe:
1/23/06 to 4/28/06
(Hand over to Process Owner)

Example of a Project Plan and Schedule

DMAIC Phase	January				February				March				April				Main Activities and Goals
	1	2	3	4	1	2	3	4	1	2	3	4	1	2	3	4	
DEFINE		▮															▶ Formulate provisional problem description and goal ▶ Draw up SIPOC ▶ Collect customer requirements ▶ Formulate project plan
MEASURE						▮											▶ Identify and define measurements ▶ Collect data ▶ Verify the problem description
ANALYZE									▮								▶ Collect possible causes ▶ Analyze process ▶ Analyze data ▶ Verify root causes
IMPROVE												▮					▶ Collect possible solutions ▶ Select solutions ▶ Elaborate action plan for implementation ▶ Test and implement solutions
CONTROL														▮			▶ Finalize documentation ▶ Implement effective, long-term monitoring system*

* If the implementation is incomplete by then, draw up a plan and coordinate with the Process Owner.

DEFINE

MEASURE

ANALYZE

IMPROVE

CONTROL

33

SIPOC

📁 **Term**
SIPOC (supplier, input, process, output, customer)

🕐 **When**
In the Define Phase, ideally at the first project meeting

◎ **Goals**
- Ensure there is a shared understanding about the process to be improved.
- Determine the relationship between customers and suppliers via the relevant process inputs and outputs.
- Identify the key customers of the process.

▶▶ **Steps**
- Fix the start and end of the underlying process.
- Draw up a rough diagram of the process to be optimized in five to seven process steps.
- Place the single process steps in their correct sequence – use a sentence with a noun and a verb.
- Identify the key inputs (what is put into the process), suppliers (who delivers the input), and outputs (the important results which the process delivers).
- Describe the key customers as receivers of the essential output. This step forms the basis for the next tool in the Define Phase.

⇨ **Tips**
- Do not depict more than the key seven steps in the SIPOC. We are dealing with a rough process description.
- When paying attention to the stop and start markers, always begin with the process. The sequence P-O-C-I-S makes sense.
- As a rule, the Project Sponsor, the Process Owner, or other stakeholders are not customers of the process.

Example SIPOC
Example: car dealer

Supplier	Input		Process		Output	Customer

START

Customer	*Vehicle*	**Receive the vehicle**
Body work	*Job*	Prepare the vehicle
Paint-supplier	*Paint*	Mix paint
		Carry out spray painting
		Drying
		Repairs / reassemble
		Deliver vehicle

Deliver vehicle → *Vehicle* | *Customer*

STOP

DEFINE

MEASURE

ANALYZE

IMPROVE

CONTROL

Customer Orientation

☐ Term
From VOC (Voice of Customer) to CTQ (Critical to Quality)

⊘ When
In the Define Phase, at the first or by the second team session at the latest

◎ Goals
- Specify the critical customer voices, which are connected with the formulated problems.
- Formulate the customer requirements (CTQ / Critical to Quality) in a clear and measurable language.

▶▶ Steps
- Adopt the key customers from the SIPOC.
- Collect the voices of the customers (VOC / Voice of Customer).
- Compress the VOCs into core statements and derive needs.
- Translate customer requirements and / or needs into the language of the process and define criteria that are critical to quality (CTQs).

⇨ Tips
- Adopt the VOCs verbatim as customer complaints, solutions, specifications and identify "true" needs.
- Categorize needs applying the Kano Model.
- Take into consideration the project goals and focus, derive the most important CTQs, maximum 5.
- With external customers use internal sources like sales & marketing or service (divisions close to the customer) for specifying the VOCs.
- Contact to external customers needs to be coordinated with sales & marketing because asking for requirements and needs usually brings with it certain expectations.
- If the project is not only driven by quality / effectiveness but Euros / efficiency, then attention should also be paid to the CTBs. Both sides of the coin are important: Efficiency and effectiveness.

Research Methods for Collecting Customer Needs

📁 **Term**

Passive and Active Research

🕐 **When**

In the Define Phase, when collecting customer needs

◎ **Goal**

Choose suitable methods in order to collect all relevant information from the customer.

▶▶ **Steps**

- Passive (internal) research in order to prepare for the active research with the customer.
- Active research methods in order to broaden and verify the assumptions.

Research Methods

Passive	Internal research	Research secondary sources on customer needs and requirements, customer values, possible product and service qualities, indicators for measuring success
Active	Going to the Gemba	Observe the customer "at work" in order to better understand his environment and activities. This method also delivers information about un-expressed needs
	1-to-1 interview	Delivers information on the needs and expectations of specific customers, the customers' values, their views about service aspects, the attributes they wish a service or product should have, and data for measuring success
	Focus group interview	The focus group is helpful for identifying the views of a group of customers. The group should represent a specific customer segment and in this way supports efforts to gain a more precise definition of the segment as well as a prioritization of customer values
	Survey	Serves to measure customer needs and values as well as the evaluation of products and services by a large number of customers from one or more segments. Based on large samples, it delivers "hard" facts for making decisions

DEFINE

MEASURE

ANALYZE

IMPROVE

CONTROL

Customer Voice Chart

📁 **Terms**

Customer Voice Chart, Customer Need Table

🕐 **When**

In the Define Phase, after the collection of customer voices

◎ **Goal**

Identify "true" customer needs

▶▶ **Steps**

– Sort collected information into the chart using the categories "Complaint", "Solution", "Specification", "Other".
– Derive the "true" needs using the information at hand.
– Formulate customer needs in a positive way: "I want …".

Derive the "True" Needs with the help of the Customer Voice Chart

Input	Solution	Specification	Other	"True" need
			It is striking that the car had an accident ⟶	I want the paint of my car to look like the original one
The paint has drained away ⟶				
I'm here to pick up my car and it isn't ready yet ⟶				I want my car to be ready by the agreed date
	The service could be friendlier ⟶			I want friendly service
		I don't want to be called because of my invoice ⟶		I want my invoice immediately

Kano Model

📁 **Term**

Kano Model*, Kano Analysis

🕐 **When**

In the Define Phase, after identifying the "true" customer needs

◎ **Goals**

– Organizing the expressed and non-expressed customer needs into "dis-satisfiers", "satisfiers", and "delighters".
– Identify those needs that have to be satisfied (mandatory) and those that can be satisfied (optional).

▶▶ **Steps**

– Every potential need is tested with the customer by posing a negatively and positively formulated question:
  - How would you feel if this need was not satisfied? (negative)
  - How would you feel if this need was satisfied? (positive)
– The customers are given four answers:
  - I like that
  - That's normal
  - I don't care
  - I don't like that
– The needs are then organized in the table based on the answers given to the negatively and positively formulated question.

⇒ **Tips**

- "Blindly" meeting articulated customer needs is very risky.
- Customers mostly articulate only "satisfiers", not "delighters" and "dis-satisfiers".
- Without an understanding of the different types of needs, the team runs the risk of:

* The model is named after its inventor Professor Noriaki Kano (Rika University, Tokio) and was developed in 1978.

- giving the process/product qualities customers are not willing to pay for;
- developing on the basis of incomplete qualities;
- developing on the basis of falsely set focal points.

Kano Table

	Answer to a negatively formulated question			
		I like that	*That's normal*	*I don't care*	*I don't like that*
Answer to a positively formulated question	*I like that*		Delighter	Delighter	Satisfier
	That's normal				Dissatisfier
	I don't care				Dissatisfier
	I don't like that				

A classification into the empty cells of the chart indicates a contradictory answer combination.

Kano Model

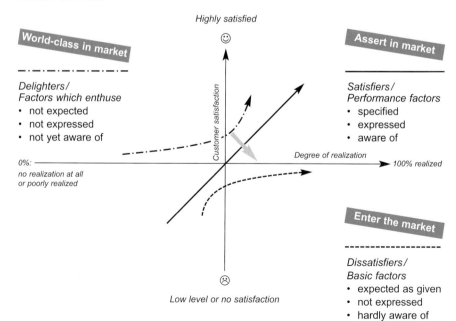

Highly satisfied

World-class in market

Delighters/
Factors which enthuse
- not expected
- not expressed
- not yet aware of

0%:
no realization at all
or poorly realized

Customer satisfaction

Degree of realization

100% realized

Assert in market

Satisfiers/
Performance factors
- specified
- expressed
- aware of

Enter the market

Dissatisfiers/
Basic factors
- expected as given
- not expressed
- hardly aware of

Low level or no satisfaction

DEFINE MEASURE ANALYZE IMPROVE CONTROL

Example: Kano Model
Example: Car dealer

- How would you feel if your car was not ready at the agreed date?
  Customer's answer: **I don't like that**

- How would you feel if your car was ready at the agreed date?
  Customer's answer: **That's normal**  Dissatisfier

- How would you feel if the service was not friendly?
  Customer's answer: **I don't like that**

- How would you feel if the service was friendly?
  Customer's answer: **I like that**  Satisfier

DEFINE

MEASURE

ANALYZE

IMPROVE

CONTROL

Tool 1: CTQ Matrix

⬚ **Term**
Tool 1: CTQ matrix (Critical to Quality)

◔ **When**
In the Define Phase, after identifying "true" customer needs

◎ **Goals**
Translating customer needs into specific, measurable customer require-ments which are critical to quality (CTQs / Critical to Quality).

▶▶ **Steps**
CTQs should be formulated in the following way:
– describing the customer requirement, not the solution
– measurable
– concise and positively formulated
– broken down into one unit of the product or the service

DEFINE

Example Tool 1: CTQ Matrix
Example: car dealer

Complaint	Solution	Specification	Other	"True" need	CTQ (critical to quality)
			It is striking that the car had an accident.	I want the paint of my car to look like the original one.	Each paint application has to correspond to the original paint with respect to coloration, thickness and density: - Thickness of paint: LSL=100µ; USL=180µ - No formation of sags and runs - Color: no visible transition
The paint has drained away.					
I'm here to pick up my car and it isn't ready yet.				I want my car to be ready by the agreed date.	Each order is completed by the agreed date.
	The service could be friendlier.			I want friendly service.	The question on friendliness in the CSI questionaire must have been answered with a grade of at least two.
		I don't want to be called because of my invoice.		I want my invoice immediately.	Each order is ready to be invoiced after the final control and the invoice can be issued immediately.

MEASURE

ANALYZE

IMPROVE

CONTROL

43

DEFINE

MEASURE

ANALYZE

IMPROVE

CONTROL

Tool 1: CTB Matrix

Term
Tool 1: CTB matrix (CTB = Critical to Business = requirements of business)

When
In the Define Phase, at the first or by the second team session at the latest and in coordination with the Sponsor

Goals
- Specify the key requirements of business, in particular for efficiency-driven projects.
- Formulate the CTBs in clear and measurable terms.

Steps
- Adopt the efficiency requirements from the project charter.
- Collect the key "Voices of Business" (VOB = Voice of Business).
- Compress the VOBs into core themes.
- Formulate measurable requirements of business (CTBs) and efficiency criteria.

Tips
- Ask the Sponsor, the Process Owner and controlling about the VOBs.
- In this context, management is not defined as a customer in the actual sense (receiver of a process output).
- The efficiency criteria of a profit-oriented company apply.

Example Tool 1: CTB Matrix
Example: car dealer

Complaint	Solution	Specification	Other	"True" need	CTBs (Critical business requirements)
The costs are too high.				I want to stick to the budget and reduce the costs of bad quality.	Reduction of rework rate from 30% to 5%.
		The mini-mum is a cost reduc-tion by 10%!			
	We need a new machine.			I want to increase my turnover.	Increase of turnover from 384,000.- € to 560,000.- €
The turn-over is decreasing.					
The costs are too high.				I want to stick to the budget and reduce the costs of bad quality.	Reduction of rework rate from 30% to 5%.
		The mini-mum is a cost reduc-tion by 10%!			

DEFINE

MEASURE

ANALYZE

IMPROVE

CONTROL

DEFINE

MEASURE

ANALYZE

IMPROVE

CONTROL

Stakeholder Analysis

☐ Term
Stakeholder analysis

◷ When
In the run-up to and for the entire duration of the project, in particular during the Define and Improve Phases (analyze possible resistance with regard to implementing improvements)

◎ Goals
– Generate support for the project.
– Identify and dispel resistance.

▶▶ Steps
1. Determine the persons relevant for a stakeholder analysis.
2. Assess these persons with regard to actual and / or expected attitudes. Mark the perceived standpoint of the person (o) and the target area (x). Visualize gaps. Plot the respective connections between the persons: who influences whom?
3. Deduce a systematic influencing strategy.

⇨ Tips
- Enter persons into the stakeholder analysis diagram, not departments.
- Confidentiality of the analysis depends on dealing openly with conflicts and resistances in the organization.

Example Stakeholder Analysis

Example: car dealer

Name	Strongly against – –	Partly against –	Neutral o	Partly pro +	Strongly pro ++
Mr. A			O		X
Mr. B	O		X		
Mr. C		O		X	

O = current state, X = target state

Example Influencing Strategy

Example: car dealer

Stakeholder	Topics/doubts	Lever	Influence (by whom)
Mr. A	Introducing SAP	Resource	Sponsor
Mr. B	Works council	Council agreement	Sponsor
Mr. C	Education	Training	Sponsor

Kick-Off Meeting

🗁 **Term**

Kick-off meeting / start workshop

🕓 **When**

First team meeting

◎ **Goals**

- Achieve the active involvement and integration of team members into the project.
- Underline and specify the importance of the topic and the project's significance for the company.
- Every team member knows and understands his role and can perform accordingly.

▶▶ **Steps**

- Coordinate the date with the Sponsor.
- Develop the agenda together with the Sponsor and the Master Black Belt.
- Invite the team members, including the wider circle.
- Arrange the room.
- Conduct the meeting in line with the defined plan.
- Compile documentation.

⇨ **Tips**

- Open the meeting. Have the Sponsor present project, problem, goal, team, etc.
- Organize suitable rooms and the necessary IT infrastructure.
- Make the agenda (with start and end times) available to the participants prior to the kick-off meeting.
- Ensure that the team members bring their work diaries so as to set the dates for follow-up meetings and absences (e.g. vacation).
- Make sure you have sufficient moderation material.

Example Kick-Off Agenda

Example: agenda

10 am	Welcome (Black Belt)
10.15 am	Introduce and present the project (Sponsor)
10.30 am	Discuss the project charter (Black Belt / Sponsor)
11 am	Six Sigma^{+Lean} introduction (Black Belt)
11.30 am	Fix roles and rules (Black Belt) Plan meetings / coordinate vacations / discuss organizational issues
12.30 pm	Lunch
1.30 pm	Develop the SIPOC (Black Belt)
2.30 pm	Determine the next steps (introductory moderation of the VOCs)
3 pm	Feedback

DEFINE

MEASURE

ANALYZE

IMPROVE

CONTROL

Gate Review

☐ Terms
Gate Review, Tollgate Review, phase check, phase transition

◔ When
At the end of each DMAIC phase

◎ Goals
- Inform the Sponsor and other stakeholders about the results achieved by the team in each phase.
- Guarantee that set goals are tracked, kept in sight and that the project is completed on time by setting and retaining the key milestones.
- Raise acceptance throughout the organization by including the key interest groups during the project.
- Evaluate and appreciate teamwork.
- Coordinate further steps and, if necessary, adjust the project scope.
- Identify risks together with the Sponsor and coordinate risk management.
- Promptly recognize if the support of the Sponsor is required.
- Decide on the continuation of the project (go/no-go).

▶▶ Steps
- Arrange the date with the Sponsor. It is recommended to include and invite the following participants at an early stage: *absolutely necessary* are the Black Belt, Sponsor, Process Owner; *optional* are the project team, quality leader, Master Black Belt, management, stakeholder, controller, internal customers.
- Prepare the presentation. The most important insights and results gained during the phase are to be made clear and the next steps are to be deduced.
- During the gate review meeting:
    - Present the phase results
    - Discuss changes and additionally necessary action, if necessary generate additional support
    - Agree on and coordinate adjustments to the project charter and project plan

- Go/no-go decision: if the decision to go ahead is made, launch the next phase; if it is decided not to go ahead as planned, discuss the steps additionally necessary to continue with the project. Alternatively, the project is cancelled.

⇒ Tips

- Coordinate gate review dates with all participants on time.
- The phase checklists for the Black Belt and Sponsor cover the key questions to be clarified and discussed during the gate review meeting.
- Besides the Black Belt, one option is to allow the team members to present the results. This will reveal to what extent the team identifies with the results and accepts working as a team.
- It is important to schedule enough time for questions and open, honest discussion.

DEFINE

MEASURE

ANALYZE

IMPROVE

CONTROL

Checklist for the Define Phase

Team
All Six Sigma^{+Lean} roles in the team are assigned. ☑

All other team members are nominated and trained in Six Sigma^{+Lean}. ☑

All project participants possess the necessary resources for the project. ☑

The capacity of team members for their project work is ensured. ☑

The team members know their roles and are aware of their function and responsibilities within the project. ☑

Project Charter
Business case, problem(s), and goal(s) are formulated SMART. ☑

Focus and scope, net benefit, milestones and project schedule are defined and agreed on. ☑

SIPOC
The process is depicted and limited to 5-7 process steps. ☑

The key outputs and the customers of the process are identified. ☑

Customers
The voices of the customer (VOCs) and business (VOBs) are collected and classified. ☑

The voices of the customer (VOCs) and business (VOBs) are translated into specific and measurable requirements. ☑

Kick-Off Meeting
The first project meeting has been held. Each team member is aware of why the project is important. ☑

Define
Carry out the Gate Review. ☑

Six Sigma^{+Lean} Toolset

MEASURE

Phase 2: Measure

Goals

- Collect data with a view to the specifications needed for meeting customer requirements.
- Ensure that measurements are accurate.
- Quantify the problems depicted in the starting situation based on figures and data on the process output.
- Use graphs and charts as a descriptive statistics to analyze the key output measurements and identify their specific characteristics.

Steps

- Determine and understand key output measurements systematically.
- Verify the accuracy using the measurement system analysis.
- Analyze the measurements in graphs and charts.
- Analyze the output measurements as to their location and spread parameters.
- Determine process capability using the process Sigma calculation and other process key figures.

Tools

- **Tool 2: Measurement Matrix**
- **Data Collection Plan**
- **Operational Definition**
- **Data Sources and Type**
- **Sample Strategy and Formulas**
- **Data Collection Forms**
- **Measurement System Analysis**
- **Gage R&R for Discrete (Binary) Data**
- **Gage R&R for Continuous Data**
- **Variation**
- **Graphs and Charts**
- **Location and Spread Parameters**
- **Process Capability Calculation**

Result from Phase 1 Define:

Tool 1: CTQ Matrix

Complaint	Solution	Specification	Other	"True" need	CTQs

Tool 2: Measurement Matrix

	Output Measurements			
CTQ/CTB				
	●	△	/	/
	/	△	●	/

Data Collection Plan

What?	How?	Who?	When?	Where?

Measurement System Analysis

No.	Operator 1		Operator 2	
	A	B	A	B
1				
2				
3				
4				

Graphs and Charts

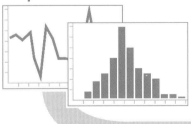

Process Capability Calculation

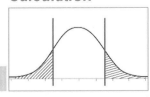

Tool 2: Measurement Matrix

☐ Terms
Tool 2: CTQ / CTB output matrix, measurement matrix

☼ When
Subsequent to tool 1

◎ Goals
- Ensure that a good output measurement is found for each CTQ / CTB.
- Select and prioritize relevant output measurements.

▶▶ Steps
- Contrast the CTQs, CTBs derived from customer and business require-ments (rows) with possible output measurements (columns).
- Evaluate how strongly the defined measurements reflect the CTQs and CTBs.

⇨ Tips
- From the customer and / or business viewpoint, ask how suitable each measurement actually is for measuring the degree of fulfilling the requirements.
- Identify for each CTQ / CTB at least one key output measurement with a strong relationship.
- Evaluate the relationship with symbols or figures (*see example*).

Example: Framing the Question
How accurately does the output measurement "paint thickness" allow us to measure the degree of fulfilling the customer requirement: "every paint application should have the thickness of the original paint between LSL = 100 μm and USL = 180 μm"?
- ● (9) Strong relationship (very high degree)
- O (3) Moderate relationship (indirect)
- Δ (1) Weak relationship (only very indirectly)
- / (0) No relationship (none at all)

Tool 2 Example: Measurement Matrix

Example: car dealer

Customer Requirements (CTQ)	Output Measurements							
	Drips and sags (Yes/no)	Colora-tion (non-defec-tive/defec-tive)	Paint-thick-ness (in micro-meters)	Paint durability (in months)	Turn-over (in €)	Mark given in CSI-survey (1-6)	Propor-tion of rework (in %)	Deviation between current and target date for hand-over (in hrs)
Every paint application should have the thickness of the original paint be-tween LSL=100 μm and USL=180 μm	/	/	●	/	/	/	○	/
Every paint application is to be free of sags and runs	●	/	/	/	/	/	○	/
Every paint application is to be even in its coloration	/	●	/	/	/	/	○	/
Every job is completed by the appointed date	/	/	/	/	/	/	○	●
Business Requirements (CTB)								
Reduce rework rate from 50% to 30%	○	○	○	○	/	△	●	/
Increase turnover from € 384,000 to € 580,000	/	/	/	/	●	/	/	/
Reduce material costs from 18.5% to 14% of turnover	/	/	○	/	/	/	/	/
Selected Output Measurements for CTQs/CTBs	✓	✓	✓		✓		✓	✓

DEFINE

MEASURE

ANALYZE

IMPROVE

CONTROL

Data Collection Plan

🗀 **Term**

Data collection plan

🕐 **When**
- Measure Phase: After tool 2: Measurement matrix
- Analyze Phase: When continuing the plan after determining the input and process measurements

◎ **Goals**
- Describe the data collection in overview: Which data is to be collected how, when, and by whom.
- Lay a foundation for the accurate collection of all relevant measurements.

▶▶ **Steps**
1. Draw up the operational definition.
2. Determine the data sources and type.
3. Devise the sample strategy.
4. Develop data collection forms.
5. Carry out the measurement system analysis.
6. Collect the data.
7. Depict the data in graphs and charts.

⇨ **Tip**

Ensure the formulation of the operational definition is in clear and precise terms.

Example Data Collection Plan
Example: car dealer

What?				How?	Who?	When?	Where?
(1)	(2)	(3)	(4)	(5)	(6)	(7)	(8)
Measure -ment	Type of measu- rement (output/ input/ process)	Type of data (con- tinuous/ discrete)	Operational definition (what)/result Gage R&R	Operational definition (how)	Respon- sible	Date/ time/ frequency	Source/ location
Colora- tion	Output	Discrete	The finished vehicle is inspected. Undercoat, paint, and varnish are applied and have dried.

Result gage R&R 90%, after rework 100%. | During visual inspection in the workshop – under full lighting ca- pacity – no difference between old and new paint applications must be visible.

The visual inspection takes place during the final control prior to handing over the vehicle to the cus- tomer. | Operator | Every second job between 1/27/2005 and 2/14/2005 | Spray- painting of vehicle |

DEFINE

MEASURE

ANALYZE

IMPROVE

CONTROL

Operational Definition

🗋 Term
Operational definition

🕑 When
After selecting the relevant measurements within the frame of data collection

◎ Goals
- Convert the theoretical requirements for collecting the measurements into specific instructions.
- Describe precisely what and how something is to be measured, so that all participants have the same understanding.

▶▶ Steps
- Formulate the operational definition specifically for every relevant output measurement (what is to be measured?).
- Describe the method for measuring (how do we measure?).
- Review the definition for shared understanding.

⇨ **Tips**
- Test the quality of the operational definition with the aid of the measurement system analysis.
- An operational definition can hint at measuring devices and tools which enable a correct evaluation like cards for comparison (e.g. for sizes and colors).

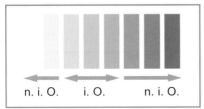

F1 ○		L1 –		B1 ——	
F2 ○		L2 —		B2 —	
F3 ◯		L3 ⋯		B3 —	
F4 ◯		L4 ———		B4 ▬	

n. i. O.   i. O.   n. i. O.

Examples of Operational Definitions

Example: Measurement: coloration of paint

Description of measurement	The color transitions from new to old paint are examined.
Measuring instrument	Visual inspection
Measurement method	The completed car is examined. Undercoat, paint and varnish were applied and dried. The visual inspection is carried out during the final control before the vehicle is handed over to the customer.
Decision criteria	During the visual inspection in the workshop – conducted with full lighting – no differences or patches between the old and the new paint are to be recognizable. Cf. color cards A37

Example: Measurement: paint thickness

Description of measurement	The paint thickness is recorded in μm.
Measuring instrument	Paint thickness - measuring instrument DFT-Ferrous (PosiTest DFT)
Measurement method	The completed vehicle is examined. Undercoat, paint and varnish were applied and dried. The device is put on the middle of the painted surface.
Decision criteria	Not applicable

DEFINE

MEASURE

ANALYZE

IMPROVE

CONTROL

Data Source Analysis

☐ Term
Data source analysis

⊘ When
Within the frame of data collection

◎ Goal
Minimize the effort needed for gathering the desired information (data) – if possible while simultaneously fulfilling the operational definition.

▶▶ Steps
Proceed according to the following priorities (see matrix below):
A Apply already existing measurements from available data sources.
B Generate newly defined measurements from existing sources.
C Look for new data sources, in order to be able to use already existing data (e.g. existing records from suppliers).
D Introduce new measurements and gain these from new data sources.

Example of Data Sources

		Measurements	
		Existing	*New*
Sources	*Existing*	**A** — Good, no time and effort needed.	**B**
	New	**C**	**D** — Poor, great time and effort needed, cost intensive.

Data Type

🗀 Term
Data type

🕑 When
Within the frame of data collection

◎ Goal
Determine the data type that allows an optimal measuring for the project / the measurement.

▶▶ Steps
– Take into consideration the measurement form, continuous or discrete: The data type determines how the data is depicted in graphs and charts, and analyzed (e.g. sample sizes are calculated differently, pie charts can only be used for discrete data).
– Favor continuous (metric) data over discrete (nominal) data: Continuous data is more accurate and thus provides a better information basis. It can deliver information about the location (mean value) and spread (standard deviation) of the measurement. Discrete data is un-able to do this.
Example of paint thickness: Non-defective or defective (discrete) ver-sus accurate paint thickness (continuous).
– In many cases metric discrete data can be treated like continuous data.

Examples of different data types are given on the following page.

DEFINE

MEASURE

ANALYZE

IMPROVE

CONTROL

Examples of Data Types

	Metric		Nominal	
Discrete	Ordinal and/or scaled to rank	Cardinal	Binary	Nominal or categories
	Examples: age, school marks, quality classes, etc.	*Example: numbers*	*Examples: male/female, heads/tails (coin), non-defective/ defective*	*Examples: color, political party, method A/B/C, telephone number*
Continuous	Cardinal		Not possible	
	Examples: temperature, weight, length, time			

⇨ **Tip**
The data type is decisive for selecting the tools (analysis of data, samples, quality key indicators, Control Charts, etc.).

Sampling Strategy

📁 **Term**
Sampling strategy

🕐 **When**
Within the frame of data collection

◎ **Goals**
– Draw meaningful conclusions from a relative small amount of data with regard to a population ("statistical conclusions/inferences").
– Save on time and effort/costs when collecting data, in particular if:
 - it is impracticable or impossible to collect and analyze all the data,
 - collecting the data turns out to be a destructive process.

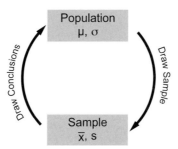

▶▶ **Steps**
The sampling strategy comprises the sampling procedure method and the planning for the sample size:
1. Determine the basis for selection (what?). This must be representative.

2. Determine the selection principle and type (how?).

3. For a random selection, determine the technique:
 - systematic selection,
 - selection through random numbers.

DEFINE

MEASURE

ANALYZE

IMPROVE

CONTROL

DEFINE

MEASURE

ANALYZE

IMPROVE

CONTROL

| | *Selection Principle* | |
	Random Selection	*Non-Random Selection*
Selection Type	• **Simple Selection** All units have the same chance of being drawn *Advantage:* No knowledge about the population necessary *Disadvantage:* Considerable effort & costs	• **Quota Procedure** Setting of quotas, e.g. damage due to accidents, repair of stone chip damage *Application:* Only when very specific information is needed
	• **Cluster Procedure** The population is subdivided into sensible clusters and one of these is selected, e.g. sites *Advantage:* Lower costs *Disadvantage:* Information can be lost	• **Concentration Procedure** Only a part of the population is observed, e.g. damage due to accidents *Application:* When only one aspect is to be examined
	• **Stratified Selection** The population is stratified according to relevant criteria, e.g. spray-paint application, shift, etc. A representative sample is then drawn from each shift. *Advantage:* Smaller samples *Disadvantage:* Information about the population must exist beforehand	• **Haphazard Selection** *Example:* Only that information is collected which is easy to acquire *Application:* When a first impression needs to be gained quickly

4. Determine the sample size.
   - The larger the sample the better.
   - Draw on all existing data when it is available (e.g. in computing system).
   - If new data is required (e.g. examination of parts/lots in production), always weigh up the costs and necessary accuracy of the measurements (granularity).

   Rule of thumb: The sample encompasses at least 30-40 (continuous) or 100 (discrete) elements, among which there must be at least 5 defective parts.

- The results of the statistical analysis indicate if larger samples are necessary. The following equations hold valid, taking into account the confidence interval:

$$\text{Discrete (binary) data} \quad n = \left\lceil \left(\frac{z}{\Delta}\right)^2 \cdot p\,(1-p) \right\rceil$$

$$\text{Continuous (metric) data} \quad n = \left\lceil \left(\frac{z \cdot s}{\Delta}\right)^2 \right\rceil$$

Here…

- Δ is half the interval breadth and +/- Δ expresses the accuracy with which the statement is to be measured (granularity).
- z is the quantile of the standard normal distribution. z can be defined through the value of 1.96 for the 95 % or 2.575 for the 99 % confidence level.
- s is the estimated standard deviation taken from a preliminary sample.
- p is the probability that a part/lot is defective (also defect rate). If the probability p is unknown, it is assumed that p = 0.5.
- n is the sample size we are looking for. The symbol $\lceil\ \rceil$ means in this case that the sample size n is rounded up to the next whole number.

⇨ **Tips**

- Statistics programs like Minitab® enable the calculation of the sample size, also allowing for the α- and ß-defect (producers or consumers risk).
- Examine data taken as samples from a population that is not yet completed, because in Six Sigma+Lean improvement projects mostly ongoing processes are observed.

An example of calculating the sample size is given on the following page.

DEFINE

Example of Calculating the Sample Size

Car dealer example: sample size for continuous data

- The drying time for the base coat is to be investigated. We want accuracy of ± 30 minutes. The drying time has a standard deviation of 2 hours.

$$n = \left\lceil \left(\frac{1.96 \cdot 2}{0.5} \right)^2 \right\rceil = \lceil 61.5 \rceil = 62$$

- The minimal sample size for this example is 62. The car dealer should ascertain at least 62 data sets.

MEASURE

Car dealer example: sample size for discrete data

- The defect rate when ordering parts is to be estimated with an accuracy of ± 5 % (Δ = 0.05).

$$n = \left\lceil \left(\frac{1.96}{0.05} \right)^2 \cdot 0.1 \cdot (1 - 0.1) \right\rceil = 139$$

- The defect rate is estimated to be around 10 % (p = 0.1).

ANALYZE

IMPROVE

CONTROL

Data Collection Forms

☐ Term
Data collection forms

⊕ When
Within the frame of data collection or whenever data is collected

◎ Goals
- Guarantee that different persons can collect the data in the same way.
- Simplify data evaluation and tracking by introducing standard data forms.

▶▶ Steps
- Draw up time-saving, simple and user-friendly forms.
- Formulate guidelines for how to fill out the forms.
- Test the form in practice.

⇨ Tips
- The quality of the data collected rises in conjunction with the quality of the forms.
- The reason for a poorly filled-out form is usually the form itself.

Example Data Collection Forms
Example 1/car dealer: tally sheet for internal rework in the paint shop

Recorded by: Meyer		Date: 4/18/2006
Reason	Frequency	Remark

1. Sags and runs, base coat:
  a. identified by customer
  b. identified by final inspection
	
	ɪɪɪɪ ɪɪɪɪ
	ɪɪɪɪ
		
		Sags and runs formed more frequently after new mix

2. No uniform paint coverage
  a. identified by customer
  b. identified by final inspection
	
	III
	ɪɪɪɪ	

Further examples of data collection forms are presented on the following page.

DEFINE

MEASURE

ANALYZE

IMPROVE

CONTROL

DEFINE

MEASURE

ANALYZE

IMPROVE

CONTROL

Example 2/car dealer: frequency chart for paint thickness

					X			
					X			
					X			
					X			
				X	X			
			X	X	X	X		
	X		X	X	X	X		X
160	161	162	163	164	165	166	167	168

Example 3

| Job Number | Closing Date | | Customer Service Employee | Reason |
	Target	Current		
10272930	Wed, 3 p.m.	Wed, 6 p.m.	BJ	Overload paint shop capacity
10272931	Wed, 6 p.m.	Wed, 6 p.m.	HP	
10272932	Thurs, midday	Thurs, 3 p.m.	CG	Dent repairs incomplete
10272933	Thurs, 3 p.m.	Thurs, 5 p.m.	BJ, BS, RB	Illness
10272934	Thurs, 3 p.m.	Thurs, 7 p.m.	CG	Overload paint shop capacity
10272935	Thurs, 6 p.m.		CG	Overload paint shop capacity
10272936	Thurs, 5 p.m.			

Example 4

Date: 4/18/05	Time: 12.15 p.m	Location: Paint store
Name: A. Meyer	Forwarder: UPS	

Damage Type	Dent	Rust	Scratch	Hole
Abb.	D	R	S	H

Left

Back

Top view

Front

Right

Measurement System Analysis

📁 **Terms**

Measurement system analysis, Gage R & R

🕐 **When**

Within the frame of data collection to check the quality of the measurement system, before data collection, Measure, Analyze, (Control)

◎ **Goals**

– Recognize, understand and minimize sources of variation that could impact on measurement result.
– Ensure a high measurement quality so that no false statements are made on the process capability.
– A reliable measurement system must satisfy the following requirements:

Accuracy / Bias

Marginal deviation between measured mean value and a standard.

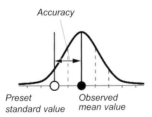

Accuracy

Preset standard value *Observed mean value*

Repeatability

Minimal fluctuations when one person measures the same unit with the same equipment.

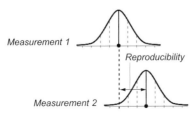

Measurement 1

Reproducibility

Measurement 2

DEFINE

MEASURE

ANALYZE

IMPROVE

CONTROL

Reproducibility

Marginal difference when several persons measure the same unit with the same equipment.

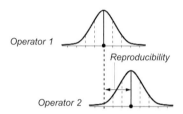

Stability

Marginal difference when the same person measures the same unit with the same equipment over a longer period.

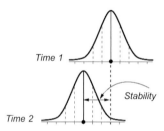

Linearity

Relationship of the bias values across the whole spectrum of the measured parts with different standard values: the bias should not change greatly by comparison when larger parts are measured (for instance weighing with a spring scale).

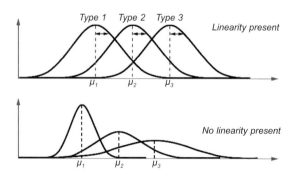

Granularity or Discrimination / Resolution

The measurement system should be able to recognize small changes or differences in the parts to be measured (a good measurement system for continuous data shoud be able to distinguish at least 5 different measurements / parts).

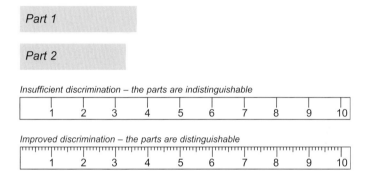

▶▶ **Steps**

1. **Preparation:** Plan the method.
   - Is the data discrete or continuous? Visual inspection or measurement? Short method or ANOVA? (Explained below)
   - Determine the number of operators for the measurement system analysis, the number of parts (sample size), and the number of repetitions by taking into account the dependence of the data type (at least 2 operators, 10 (30) samples for continuous (discrete) data, 2 repeats).

2. **Execution:** Collect the data.
   - Discrete data: Gage R & R
   - Continuous data: Gage R & R ANOVA

3. **Data analysis:** Interpret the results.

⇨ **Tips**

- Emphasize the border line parts (just-in and just-out about good or poor enough) when selecting the sample.
- Select a measuring instrument so that the accuracy amounts to at least 1/10 of the expected variation.

DEFINE

MEASURE

ANALYZE

IMPROVE

CONTROL

Gage R & R for Discrete (Binary) Data

☐ Term
Gage R & R for discrete (binary) data

☉ When
Within the frame of data collection to check the quality of the measurement system, before data collection, Measure, Analyze, (Control)

◎ Goals
– Ensure that the data collection is repeatable and reproducible.
– Verify the operational definition.

▶▶ Steps
– Name the expert who is to set the standard.
– Name the operators and provide the parts / items to be examined. As a rule, 2 persons and at least 30 samples are required.
– All parts to be examined must be numbered.
– Determine the standard based on the expert's visual inspection. Record the results on a sheet, e.g. non-defective / defective.
– Visual inspection by the first operator.
– Visual inspection by the second operator.
– Repeat the procedure without looking at the results one has already taken, those of the experts, or the other operator. The sequence of the parts in the visual inspections should be changed randomly to ensure this.
– Always note down the sequence of the parts – paginate.
– Check for matches. The goal with a good measurement system: 100 %. A match of at least 90 % with respect to results in evaluations can be viewed as acceptable.
– Examine the reasons for possible deviations.
– If the result is below 90 %:
  - Review the operational definition and redefine if necessary.
  - Provide operators with more intensive coaching.
  - Identify and eliminate disruptive noise factors.

⇒ **Tips**

- Instead of consulting a single expert, it makes more sense in practice to call on a panel of experts. This panel of experts should include the customers of the process, e.g. final assembly, and the end user, or at least an internal representative, e.g. quality management.
- Ideally, it is better to have the whole inspectors team involved in the Gage R & R and not just two operators.
- Ensure the easy review of the results through a thorough documentation of the expert decisions in visuals and writing. This also helps to realize targeted improvements and to implement necessary adjustments.

Example Gage R & R for Discrete Data

Example / car dealer: setup for data collection Gage R & R (binary data)

Number	Standard / experts	Operator 1		Operator 2		Matching (y/n)
		Recording I	*Recording II*	*Recording I*	*Recording II*	
1	Non-defective	Non-defective	Non-defective	Non-defective	Non-defective	Y
2	Defective	Defective	Defective	Defective	Defective	Y
3	Non-defective	Non-defective	Non-defective	Non-defective	Non-defective	Y
4	Non-defective	Non-defective	Defective	Non-defective	Non-defective	N
5	Non-defective	Non-defective	Defective	Non-defective	Non-defective	N
6	Defective	Defective	Defective	Defective	Defective	Y
7	Non-defective	Non-defective	Non-defective	Non-defective	Non-defective	Y
...	...	...	...	...	...	...
29	Non-defective	Non-defective	Non-defective	Defective	Defective	N
30 etc.	Non-defective	Non-defective	Non-defective	Non-defective	Non-defective	Y
% compliance with standard		83.3 %		96.67 %		
% Repeatability		80 %		100 %		
% Reproducibility						90 %

No repeatability! *   *No reproducibility!*

* *Should allways be checked first: if there is no repeatability there is also no reproducibility*

Gage R & R ANOVA for Continuous Data

🗀 Term
Gage R & R ANOVA for continuous data

🕓 When
Within the frame of data collection to check the quality of the measurement system, before data collection, Measure, Analyze, (Control)

◎ Goal
Ensure that the measurement process is repeatable and reproducible.

▶▶ Steps
– Select a measuring instrument so that the accuracy amounts to at least 1/10 of the expected variation.
– Name the operators and provide the parts to be examined. As a rule, 2 persons and at least 30 samples are required.
– The parts are numbered.
– 1st operator carries out the first measurement.
– 2nd operator carries out the first measurement.
– Repeat the procedure without the operators seeing their results or those of their counterparts. The sequence of the parts in the measurement should be changed randomly.
– Always note down the sequence of the parts – paginate.
– Enter the results in Minitab® and select Gage R & R ("crossed"). For destructive measurements (e.g. crash test) select the Gage R & R study "nested".
– Analyze the results.

Attention: Do not "favorably calculate" the result of the P/T ratio by extending the tolerance (USL – LSL).

What is required if the result is unacceptable?
– Review the operational definition and redefine if necessary.
– Provide the operators with more intensive coaching.
– Check the measuring equipment and optimize if necessary.

Example of a Decision Matrix for Gage R & R – Continuous (Metric) Data

			Acceptable Result	More Accuracy Needed	Unacceptable Result
Without Specification Limits	% Gage (% Contribution)	$\dfrac{s^2_{Gage}}{s^2_{Total}} \cdot 100$	< 1 %	< 9 %	> 9 %
	% Study Variation (% SV)	$\dfrac{s_{Gage}}{s_{Total}} \cdot 100$	< 10 %	< 30 %	> 30 %
With Specification Limits	% P/T-Ratio	$\dfrac{5.15 \cdot s^2_{Gage}}{Tolerance} \cdot 100$	< 10 %	< 30 %	> 30 %

Source: Automotive Industry Action Group (AIAG)

Gage R & R for Continuous Data

Example: Gage R & R ANOVA Method

```
Gage R&R
                             %Contribution
Source              VarComp  (of VarComp)
Total Gage R&R        1.48        0.11
Repeatability         0.68        0.05
Reproducibility       0.81        0.06
Operator              0.03        0.00
Operator*vehicle      0.78        0.06
Part-To-Part       1395.86       99.89
Total Variation    1397.34      100.00

                                Study Var  %Study Var
Source             StdDev (SD)  (5.15 * SD)   (%SV)
Total Gage R&R        1.2185        6.275      3.26
Repeatability         0.8216        4.231      2.20
Reproducibility       0.8998        4.634      2.41
Operator              0.1620        0.834      0.43
Operator*vehicle      0.8851        4.558      2.37
Part-To-Part         37.3612      192.410     99.95
Total Variation      37.3810      192.512    100.00

Number of Distinct Categories = 43

Gage R&R for measurement
```

Analytical result:
Only 0.11 % of the whole variation is caused by the measurement system, namely through repeatability (0.05 %) and reproducibility (0.06 %). If no tolerance ranges (specification limits) were given, then a maximum of 4 % contribution and 20 % SV are admissible.

We should be able to distinguish between at least 5 categories. A lower number of distinctive categories indicates a weak measurement system, because differences between the parts cannot be recognized.

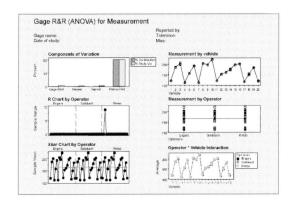

DEFINE · MEASURE · ANALYZE · IMPROVE · CONTROL

DEFINE

MEASURE

Example: Gage R & R ANOVA Method

Gage R&R

		%Contribution
Source	VarComp	(of VarComp)
Total Gage R&R	1.48	0.11
Repeatability	0.68	0.05
Reproducibility	0.81	0.06
Operator	0.03	0.00
Operator*vehicle	0.78	0.06
Part-To-Part	1395.86	99.89
Total Variation	1397.34	100.00

		Study Var	%Study Var	%Tolerance
Source	StdDev (SD)	(6 * SD)	(%SV)	(SV/Toler)
Total Gage R&R	1.2185	7.311	3.26	9.14
Repeatability	0.8216	4.930	2.20	6.16
Reproducibility	0.8998	5.399	2.41	6.75
Operator	0.1620	0.972	0.43	1.22
Operator*vehicle	0.8851	5.311	2.37	6.64
Part-To-Part	37.3612	224.167	99.95	280.21
Total Variation	37.3810	224.286	100.00	280.36

Number of Distinct Categories = 43

Gage R&R for measurement

Analytical result:
% P/T ratio (% tolerances) indicates the measuring error as depending on the given tolerance.

The P/T ratio should not exceed 20%.

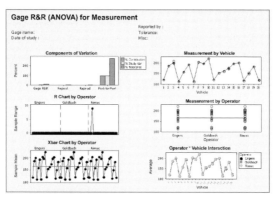

Results in graphs and charts: the 3 measures % contribution, % SV, and % P/T ratio are depicted.

ANALYZE

IMPROVE

CONTROL

Variation

📁 **Terms**

Variation-based thinking, understanding variation

🕑 **When**

In the Measure and Control Phases, always after collecting data

◎ **Goals**

- – Visualize data.
- – Develop a feeling for the collected data and its distribution.
- – Recognize outliers and patterns.
- – Assess the location and spread.
- – Assess how well the current process satisfies requirements.
- – Identify the first signs of causes for variation.

▶▶ **Steps**

1. Depict the data in graphs and charts.
2. Analyze the statistical key figures.

DEFINE

MEASURE

ANALYZE

IMPROVE

CONTROL

Pie Chart

☐ Term
Pie Chart

◷ When
In the Measure Phase after collecting data, later after every data collection

◎ Goal
Depict discrete data according to frequency.

▶▶ Step
Depict the relative frequency (percentages/proportion) of a discrete (metric or nominal) characteristic in a "pie"-shaped chart. The whole pie covers 100% of the data.

Example of a Pie Chart

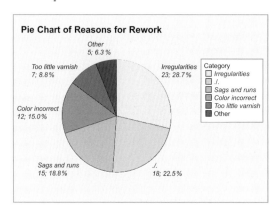

Pie Chart of Reasons for Rework

Other
5; 6.3%

Too little varnish
7; 8.8%

Irregularities
23; 28.7%

Color incorrect
12; 15.0%

Sags and runs
15; 18.8%

./.
18; 22.5%

Category
☐ Irregularities
☐ ./.
☐ Sags and runs
☐ Color incorrect
☐ Too little varnish
☐ Other

Result:
The sizes of the "pie pieces" represent the proportional share of the whole. Pie charts show the relationship between amounts by dividing the whole "pie" (100%) into pieces or smaller percentages.

⇨ Tip
Begin with the largest percentage segment at "12 o'clock" and proceed in a clockwise direction.

Pareto Chart

☐ Term
Pareto chart

◔ When
In the Measure Phase after collecting data, later after every data collection

◎ Goals
- Depict the focal points and thus set priorities for discrete data.
- Concentrate on those vital few causes whose optimization will generate the greatest impact (80:20 rule).

▶▶ Steps
- Depict the data in categories.
- Add up the frequencies of the individual categories so as to select the correct standard on the Y-axis in the Pareto chart.
- Depict the bars representing the categories true to scale: From left to right according to their frequency and in descending order of importance.
- Depict the curve that shows the cumulative frequency.

⇢ **Tips**
- Ensure that the category "other" – if existent – is small.
- It helps considerably when just a few categories make up the greater part of the problem.

An example of a Pareto chart is given on the following page.

DEFINE

MEASURE

ANALYZE

IMPROVE

CONTROL

Example Pareto Chart

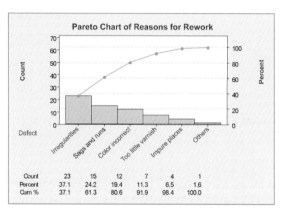

Dot Plot

📁 **Term**
Dot plot

🕐 **When**
In the Measure Phase after collecting data, later after every data collection

◎ **Goals**
- Depict the spread of continuous data in a simple way.
- Identify outliers, in particular with smaller data amounts.

▶▶ **Steps**
- Depict the frequencies in single data dots.
  (Minitab® begins automatically to form classes for large data amounts with several decimal places)
- Every value is recorded as a single dot in the plot.

⇨ **Tip**
A dot plot can also be used to determine if the sample scope is large enough: An expert recognizes whether the whole data spread is depicted or if additional data is necessary.

Example of a Dot Plot

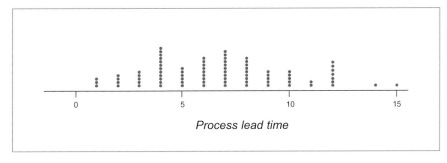

Process lead time

DEFINE

MEASURE

ANALYZE

IMPROVE

CONTROL

DEFINE

MEASURE

ANALYZE

IMPROVE

CONTROL

Histogram

📁 **Term**

Histogram, frequency chart

🕐 **When**

In the Measure Phase after collecting data, later after every data collection

◎ **Goals**
- Depict the distribution of continuous data.
- With this aid, find out if a process is centered in relation to customer requirements and if the spread lies within the specification limits.

▶▶ **Steps**
- Summarize continuous data in categories or classes.
  Rule of thumb: Number of categories (c) is $c = \sqrt{n}$.
- Record the frequencies of actually occurring categories in bars true to scale. The relevant interval for the data to be depicted stands on the x-axis. The frequencies are on the y-axis (absolute or relative percentage values).

⇒ **Tips**
- Use larger data sets (at least 50-100 data points). Data sets that are too small can end in misleading interpretations.
- Several peaks in a histogram may indicate that the data set is too small or that the data comes from different sources. If this is the case, stratify or layer the data set. Other forms of distribution and actions resulting from this are described in the following.

Example Histogram

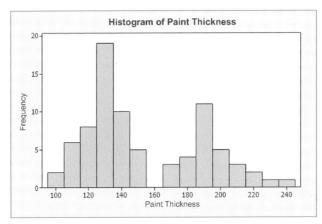

Forms of distribution

Process A
Symmetric, bell-curve distribution

Process B
Bimodal distribution; the data probably comes from several sources or, as in this case, from two different processes

Process C
Positive or right-skewed distribution

Process D
Negative or left-skewed distribution

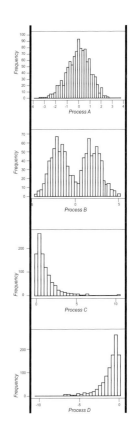

DEFINE

MEASURE

ANALYZE

IMPROVE

CONTROL

Centering and Spread, Customer Requirements, Specification Limits

Process 1

Centered and fully within the customer specifications

→ Maintain this state

Process 2

Customer specifications are just about met; high defect risk

→ Reduce the spread

Process 3

Spread is low, but the target value is not met, and so the customer specification is not fulfilled

→ Center the process

Process 4

Process is centered but spread too big

→ Reduce the spread

Process 5

Process is not centered and spread too big

→ Reduce spread and then center the process

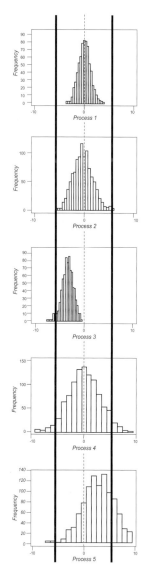

Box Plot

📁 Terms
Box and whisker plot

🕐 When
After collecting data, in particular when stratifying data

◎ Goals
- Depict the location and spread of a continuous data set.
- Undertake a quicker comparison of different data sets (e.g. compare suppliers, machinery).
- Summarize a data set in graphs and charts, featuring the median, the 1st and 3rd quartile (which amount to 25 % and 75 % of the data, respectively), and the extreme values.

▶▶ Steps
1. Record the maximum and minimum values true to scale and connect them with a vertical line.
2. Depict the median as a horizontal.
3. Plot a box between the 1st and 3rd quartile.

⇢ Tips
- Box Plots are an excellent tool for comparing several data sets. In this case each box plot depicts one data set.
- As a rule, statistics programs plot outliers separately.

An example of a box plot is given on the following page.

DEFINE

MEASURE

ANALYZE

IMPROVE

CONTROL

DEFINE

MEASURE

ANALYZE

IMPROVE

CONTROL

Example of a Box Plot
Summary of a data set

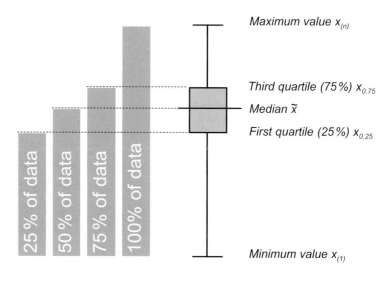

Maximum value $x_{(n)}$

Third quartile (75%) $x_{0.75}$
Median $\tilde{x}$
First quartile (25%) $x_{0.25}$

25% of data
50% of data
75% of data
100% of data

Minimum value $x_{(1)}$

Run Chart

📁 **Terms**
Run chart, time series plot

🕐 **When**
In the Measure Phase after collecting data, later after every data collection, in particular in the Control Phase

◎ **Goals**
– Depict trends, shifts or patterns in a process with continuous or discrete data.
– Compare the process flow before and after improvement.

▶▶ **Steps**
– Plot the relevant period on the x-axis and the observed characteristic of the process on the y-axis.
– Assign a corresponding value to every defined point in time.
– Connect plotted values with a line.

Example of a Run Chart

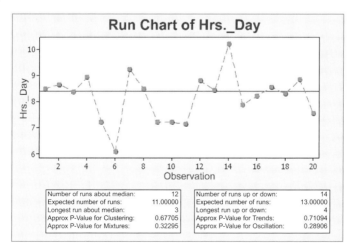

Number of runs about median: 12	Number of runs up or down: 14
Expected number of runs: 11.00000	Expected number of runs: 13.00000
Longest run about median: 3	Longest run up or down: 4
Approx P-Value for Clustering: 0.67705	Approx P-Value for Trends: 0.71094
Approx P-Value for Mixtures: 0.32295	Approx P-Value for Oscillation: 0.28906

DEFINE

MEASURE

ANALYZE

IMPROVE

CONTROL

⇨ **Tips**

- At least 20 data points are required, to be able to recognize a meaningful pattern.
- The data sequence corresponds to the time order of its collection.
- The following examples display possible patterns and their interpretations as well as actions to be taken.

Run Chart	Description	Interpretation	Action
	Too little data points	Little clusters (accumulation of points) above or below the median may indicate a cycle	Analyze what the clusters below the median have in common and how they differ from those above the median
	Too many data points	Too many clusters above or below the median indicate overcompensation, a sample taken from several sources, or contrived data	Analyze what distinguishes the upper from the lower points
	Shifts	Eight or more successive points on one side of the median indicate a shift in a key element of the process	Analyze what was changed in the process at the moment when the shift emerged
	Trends	Seven or more points which rise or fall continuously indicate a trend	Analyze which strong factor has caused the change / trend
	Same values	A succession of seven or more points with the same value	Analyze if the measuring equipment has become "stuck"

DEFINE

MEASURE

ANALYZE

IMPROVE

CONTROL

Control Charts

☐ Terms
Control charts, Shewart charts

⏱ When
In the Measure Phase after collecting data, later after every data collection, in particular in the Control Phase

◎ Goals
- Review process stability following the data collection.
- Monitor the process in the Control Phase.
- Determine in the Measure phase if special or common causes for variation are to be located in the Analyze Phase.

The Control charts are presented in detail in the "Control" section.

DEFINE

MEASURE

ANALYZE

IMPROVE

CONTROL

Scatter Plot

☐ **Term**
Scatter plot

⏱ **When**
At the end of the Measure Phase as an outlook on the Analyze Phase, and in particular in the Analyze Phase itself

◎ **Goal**
Depict a (linear or non-linear) relationship between two metric variables.

▶▶ **Step**
Plot the data points, which represent the value of one dimension (x-axis) and the corresponding value of another dimension (y-axis).

⇨ **Tips**
- This is another possibility for verifying the suspected relationships from the cause-and-effect diagram.
- Scatter Plots do not necessarily illustrate a cause-effect relation. They merely show that a relationship exists.

Example Scatter Plot

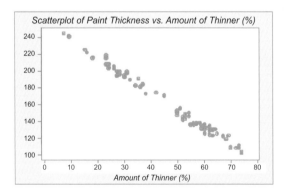

Normal Probability Plot

📁 **Term**

Normal probability plot

🕐 **When**

At the end of the Measure Phase, after every data collection

◎ **Goal**

Check the data set for normal distribution, which is important for determining the process performance figures.

▶▶ **Steps**

– Transform the distribution function of the (theoretical) normal distribution so that it represents a straight line. Given the complexity of this transformation, create a normal probability plot with the aid of statistical software.
– Record the data points of the empirical distribution (existing data set).
– If necessary, depict a confidence interval.
– If the data points lie on the straight line or within the confidence interval, we may assume that the data is normal.

⇨ **Tip**

The result of the test for normal distribution presented in the statistics software Minitab® is based on the Anderson-Darling test.

An example of a normal probability plot is given on the following page.

DEFINE

MEASURE

ANALYZE

IMPROVE

CONTROL

DEFINE

MEASURE

ANALYZE

IMPROVE

CONTROL

Example of a Normal Probability Plot

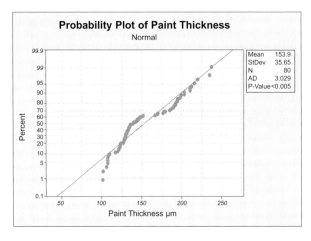

Location Parameter: Mean

📁 **Terms**
Mean, mean value, arithmetic mean

🕐 **When**
After every data collection

◎ **Goal**
Determine the position of a set of continuous data.

▶▶ **Step**
Form the sum of all data and divide it by the number of data points (n).

$$\bar{x} = \frac{\sum_{j=1}^{n} x_j}{n} = \frac{x_1 + x_2 + \ldots + x_n}{n}$$

⇨ **Tip**
$\bar{x}$ is used for the mean value of a sample; if the mean value of a population is determined, the sign μ is used.

Example of a Mean

Example:
The sample of paint thickness after repairs with the sample size six resulted in the following results (in micro-meters): 255, 89, 110, 152, 324 and 199.

$$\bar{x} = \frac{255 + 89 + 110 + 152 + 324 + 199}{6} = 188.17$$

DEFINE

MEASURE

ANALYZE

IMPROVE

CONTROL

Location Parameter: Median

📁 **Term**
Median

🕐 **When**
After every data collection

◎ **Goal**
Determine the location of a data set.

▶▶ **Steps**
- Sort the data in ascending order
- Determine the median:
  - With an *uneven* number of data by determining the data point in the middle

$$\tilde{x} = x_{\left(\frac{n+1}{2}\right)}$$

  - With an *even* number of data by forming the mean value of both data in the middle.

$$\tilde{x} = \frac{1}{2}\left(x_{(n/2)} + x_{\left(\frac{n}{2}+1\right)}\right)$$

The median divides the data set, whereby one half of the data lies above the median, the other below.

⇨ **Tip**
The median is less sensitive to outliers than the mean value. In this case, the median is more likely to show the real location of the majority of data from a data set.

Example of a Median

Uneven sample size   62, 89, 110, 152, 199, 255, 324
                                    x_{50} *(Median)*

Even sample size   89, 110, 152, 199, 255, 324 $\tilde{x} = \dfrac{152 + 199}{2} = 175.5$
                                x_{50} *(Median)*

Location Parameter: Mode

📁 **Term**
Mode, modal value

🕐 **When**
After every data collection

◎ **Goal**
Determine the location of a data set.

▶▶ **Steps**
- Determine the frequency of each value.
- The modal value corresponds to the value of the data set that appears most frequently.

⇨ **Tips**
- If there are two modal values we speak of a bimodal data set. This can indicate two different populations.
- Determining the modal value only makes sense with metric, discrete data, because the single data points usually occur only once with con-tinuous data.

Example of Mode
The following data was collected for the lead time of jobs at the car dealer:

Modal value

Days	1	2	3	4	5	6	7	8	9	10	11	12	13	14	15
Fre-quency	3	4	5	**12**	6	9	10	9	5	5	2	6	0	1	1

DEFINE

MEASURE

ANALYZE

IMPROVE

CONTROL

Spread Parameter: Variance

📁 **Term**
Variance

🕐 **When**
After every data collection

◎ **Goal**
Depict the spread of a process (the greater the variance the greater the spread of a process).

▶▶ **Steps**
- Form the sum of the squared deviations of all data from the mean value and then divide by the number of data points minus one (n‑1)
- The resulting variance is the average, squared deviation from the mean value

$$s^2 = \frac{\sum_{j=1}^{n}(x_j - \bar{x})^2}{n-1} = \frac{(x_1 - \bar{x})^2 + (x_2 - \bar{x})^2 + \ldots + (x_n - \bar{x})^2}{n-1}$$

⇢ **Tip**
The variance is difficult to interpret due to the squared dimension. It plays, however, an important role in statistical tests.

Example of Variance

$$s^2 = \frac{(255 - 188.17)^2 + (89 - 188.17)^2 + \ldots}{6-1} = \frac{40{,}286.83}{5} = 8{,}057.37$$

Spread Parameter: Standard Deviation

📁 **Term**

Standard deviation

🕐 **When**

After every data collection

◎ **Goal**

Depict the spread of a process (the greater the standard deviation the greater the spread of a process).

▶▶ **Step**

Form the square root from the variance. The resulting value matches the standard deviation.

$$s = \sqrt{\frac{\sum\limits_{j=1}^{n}(x_j - \bar{x})^2}{n-1}}$$

⇨ **Tips**

- The standard deviation has the same dimension as the data set or the mean value and is thus easier to interpret.
- The standard deviation is the most common measure for quantifying variation.
- s stands for the standard deviation of a sample, σ for the standard deviation of the population.

Example of a Standard Deviation

$$s = \sqrt{8{,}057.37} = 89.76$$

DEFINE

MEASURE

ANALYZE

IMPROVE

CONTROL

Spread Parameter: Range

☐ **Term**
Range

🕓 **When**
After every data collection

◎ **Goal**
Depict the spread of a process (the greater the range the greater the spread of the process).

▶▶ **Step**
Form the difference between the largest and smallest value of a data set. This difference matches the range.

$$R = x_{max.} - x_{min.}$$

⇢ **Tip**
The range is sensitive to outliers and therefore requires careful interpretation.

Example of Range

$$R = 324 - 89 = 235$$

Span

☐ Terms
Span, percentile span

☽ When
After every data collection

◎ Goal
Depict the spread of a data set, which was purified of outliers.

▶▶ Steps
- Sort the data according to size, as a rule in ascending order.
- Remove for example the smallest 5% and the largest 5% of the data from the data set.
- The span (90) is the range purified of the outliers (5% from both sides).

$$\text{Span (90)} = x_{0.95} - x_{0.05}$$

⇨ Tip
See Process Performance on the following page.

Example of Span

$n = 100$, min. $= 100$, max. $= 300$, $P_{0.05} = 110$, $P_{0.95} = 255$

$$\text{Span (90)} = 255 - 110 = 145$$

Process Performance

☐ Term
Process performance, process capability

⊙ When
Phase closure Measure, continuously during Analyze and Improve, and in particular in the Control Phase.

◎ Goals
– Determine the performance capability of a process in terms of customer requirements
– Describe the status quo and the improvements achieved after implementing solutions

▶▶ Step
The quality key figures usually used in the world of Six Sigma^{+Lean} to determine the performance capability are:

DPMO	Defects per million opportunities
ppm	Parts per million
DPU	Defects per unit
Yield	Output of a process
Span	Percentile distance of deviations from target value
C_p and C_{pk}	Process capability indexes
Process Sigma	"Sigma value"

Defects Per Million Opportunities (DPMO)

📂 **Term**
Defects per million opportunities

🕑 **When**
Phase closure Measure, continuously during the Analyze, Improve and Control Phases and after the completion of the project to secure sustainability

◎ **Goal**
Focus on the internal view of minimizing the number of defects per unit.

▶▶ **Steps**
- Define the produced unit (output of a process, e.g. a spray-painting job).
- Determine the defect opportunities (as a rule derived from the CTQs).
- Define the defects (every defect opportunity occurring in a unit corresponds to a defect).
- Determine the number of inspected units and count the defects.
- Calculate the DPMO value, where:
  D = the total number of defects,
  N = the number of processed units,
  O = the number of defect opportunities:

$$\text{DPMO} = \frac{D}{N \cdot O} \cdot 1{,}000{,}000$$

⇒ **Tips**
- Describe only those defect opportunities which are derived from the CTQs and actually occur as a defect.
- When counting the defects, ensure that the unit is checked for all defect opportunities.
- The Sigma conversion table lists the process Sigma (Sigma value).
- The number of defect opportunities should match the number of CTQs

An example of a DPMO calculation is given on the following page.

Example of DPMO

Example (main operations): calculating the process Sigma

1. Number of units to be processed $\quad\quad\quad\quad\quad$ N $\;=\;$ 80

2. Total number of defects
   (including defects corrected later) $\quad\quad\quad\quad$ D $\;=\;$ 108

3. Number of defect opportunities $\quad\quad\quad\quad\quad$ O $\;=\;$ 4

4. Equation for defects per million opportunities $\quad$ DPMO $\;=\; \dfrac{D}{N \cdot O} \cdot 10^6$

   $\quad\quad\quad\quad\quad\quad\quad\quad\quad\quad\quad\quad\quad\quad\quad\quad\quad = \dfrac{108}{80 \cdot 4} \cdot 10^6$

   $\quad\quad\quad\quad\quad\quad\quad\quad\quad\quad\quad\quad\quad\quad\quad\quad\quad = 337{,}500$

5. Look up the process Sigma in the abridged
   conversion table $\quad\quad\quad\quad\quad\quad\quad\quad$ $\text{Sigma}_{(ST)}$ $\;=\;$ 1.95

104

Parts Per Million (ppm)

☐ Term
Parts per million (ppm)

☷ When
Phase closure Measure, continuously during the Analyze, Improve and Control Phases and after the completion of the project to secure sustainability

◎ Goal
Focus on the customer's viewpoint: A unit with one defect and a part with several defects are equally defective and are counted as a defect because the unit is all in all useless for the customer.

▶▶ Steps
- Determine the defect opportunities for which, when they occur, a whole unit is marked as defective.
- Determine the number of inspected units and count the defects and/or defective units.
- Calculate the ppm value:

$$\text{ppm} = \frac{\text{number of defective units}}{\text{total number of units}} \cdot 1,000,000$$

⇨ Tip
If there is only one single defect opportunity the DPMO corresponds to the ppm value.

Example of ppm
Example: parts per million

- Due to defects in paint work, rework was required for 63 out of 80 jobs and/or the jobs were not completed on time:

$$\text{ppm} = \frac{63}{80} \cdot 1,000,000 = 787,500$$

- We have a ppm rate in the main operations of 787,500.

DEFINE

MEASURE

ANALYZE

IMPROVE

CONTROL

Defects Per Unit (DPU)

📁 **Term**
Defects per unit (DPU)

🕐 **When**
Phase closure Measure, continuously during the Analyze, Improve and Control Phases and after the completion of the project to secure sustainability

◎ **Goal**
Determine the average number of defects per unit.

▶▶ **Steps**
– Define the defects (every defect opportunity occurring in a unit corresponds to a defect).
– Determine the number of inspected units and count the defects.
– Calculate the DPU value:
$$DPU = \frac{\text{total number of defects}}{\text{total number of units}}$$

⇨ **Tip**
Taken together, the three quality key figures DPMO, ppm and DPU provide a comprehensive picture of process performance – it is recommended to use all three figures!

Example of DPU
Example: defects per unit

- A total number of 108 defects were identified in 80 jobs at the main operation:

$$DPU = \frac{108}{80} = 1.35$$

- We have a DPU rate of 1.35. This means that on average <u>one</u> produced part has 1.35 defects.

Yield

📁 **Term**
Yield

🕐 **When**
Phase closure Measure, continuously during the Analyze, Improve and Control Phases and after the completion of the project to secure sustainability

◎ **Goal**
Determine the proportion of good parts in a process.

▸▸ **Steps**
- **Yield:** Reflects the proportion of good units.

$$Y = \frac{\text{number of non-defective units}}{\text{total number of units}}$$

  – Connection between DPU and Yield (with assumed Poisson distribution):

$$Y = e^{-DPU}$$

  – Connection between DPO and Yield:

$$Y = 1 - DPO \text{ whereby } DPO = \frac{D}{N \cdot O}$$

- **Rolled throughput yield:** Determines the probability that a unit runs through the entire process without defects. The total yield is calculated by multiplying the single sub-process yields.

$$Y_{RTP} = Y_{Sub\,1} \cdot Y_{Sub\,2} \cdot \ldots \cdot Y_{Sub\,n}$$

- **Normalized yield:** Determines the average yield per process step. *Attention:* This measure can be misleading if the yields in the single process steps vary greatly.

$$Y_{Norm} = \sqrt[n]{Y_{RTP}}$$

DEFINE

MEASURE

ANALYZE

IMPROVE

CONTROL

DEFINE

MEASURE

ANALYZE

IMPROVE

CONTROL

⇨ **Tips**

- We can distinguish between two characteristics of the yield:
  1. Production of parts: Percentage of good units in relation to the total amount of units produced (yield in the classical production).
  2. Chemistry industry: Amount of finished material in relation to the amount of raw material.
- As a rule, identify the yield before any improvements or post-processing or rework occur (first-pass yield).

Examples of Yield

Example 1: car dealer yield

- Only 21 out of 80 spray-painting jobs were without defects.
- We have a yield rate of 26.25 %.

$$\text{Yield} = \frac{21}{80} = 0.2625 = 26.25\,\%$$

Example 2: car dealer throughput yield

- There was a total of 108 defects out of 80 spray-painting jobs in the process. The DPU was 1.35. How high is the yield (if the defects are not distributed equally)?

$$Y_{TP} = e^{-1.35} = 0.2592 = 25.92\,\%$$

- This means that the proportion of non-defective parts is 25.92 %.

Example 3: car dealer rolled throughput yield

- The following yields are calculated for the single process steps:

$$Y_1 = 92\,\% \rightarrow Y_2 = 82\,\% \rightarrow Y_3 = 84\,\% \rightarrow Y_4 = 82\,\% \rightarrow Y_5 = 95\,\%$$

- The probability that a unit runs through the entire process without defects is:

$$Y_{RTP} = 0.92 \cdot 0.82 \cdot 0.84 \cdot 0.82 \cdot 0.95 \cong 0.494$$

Overall Equipment Effectiveness

🗀 **Term**

Overall Equipment Effectiveness, OEE

🕓 **When**

In the Measure, Analyze, Improve and Control Phases

◎ **Goal**

– Understand equipment effectiveness.
– Determine the percentage of time in which an equipment component produces quality products with a given takt rate.

▶▶ **Steps**

1. **Calculate the components of OEE**

OEE or Overall Equipment Effectiveness

Availability Level (AL)	Performance Level (PL)	Quality Level (QL)
• **Equipment breakdown** Mechanical, pneumatic or hydraulic defects which result in production losses. • **Losses due to setup** Equipment is set up for the production of a new part.	• **Idle time and short stops** Time in which equipment runs without producing anything as well as short-term interruptions or breakdowns of equipment. • **Reduced takt rate** Equipment is not operated with the scheduled takt rate.	• **Quality losses** Activities connected with quality assurance of a product (scrap and rework). Rework often means that the part has to go through the entire production step again.

DEFINE

MEASURE

ANALYZE

IMPROVE

CONTROL

Scheduled busy time		T = Total no. of hours in operation [h]				
Availability level (AL)	$AL = \dfrac{A}{T} \cdot 100\%$	A = Availability [h]	Equipment, outages	Setup and equipping	Idle	
Performance level (PL)	$PL = \dfrac{S}{T} \cdot 100\%$	S = Max. Takt speed [h]	Speed loss			
Quality level (QL)	$QL = \dfrac{Q}{T} \cdot 100\%$	Q = Good quality [h]	Rework, scrap/ reject			

Availability level (AL)	$AL = \dfrac{T_{Run}}{T_B} \cdot 100\%$	T_B = Scheduled busy time [h]
		T_{Run} = Machinery run time [h]
		T_{Cons} = Processing time at constraint [h/unit]
Performance level (PL)	$PL = \dfrac{T_{Cons} \cdot N_{Finished}}{T_{Run}} \cdot 100\%$	N_{Good} = No. of good parts completed [unit]
		$= N_{Finished} - N_{Scrap} - N_{Rework}$
Quality level (QL)	$QL = \dfrac{N_{Good}}{N_{Finished}} \cdot 100\%$	N_{Scrap} = No. of scrap
		N_{Rework} = No. of parts for rework
		$N_{Finished}$ = Total no. of finished goods

2. Calculate the OEE

OEE	$OEE = AL \cdot PL \cdot QL$

$$OEE = \underbrace{\frac{T_{Run}}{T_B}}_{\text{Availability level}} \cdot \underbrace{\frac{T_{Cons} \cdot N_{Good}}{T_{Run}}}_{\text{Performance level}} \cdot \underbrace{\frac{N_{Good} - N_{Scrap} - N_{Rework}}{N_{Finished}}}_{\text{Quality level}}$$

Example of OEE

Example	$OEE = 73\% \cdot 91\% \cdot 80\%$ $= 53\%$

80% *World-class, depending on branch*

Span / Percentile Distance

☐ Terms

Span, percentile distance (of the deviations from the target value as a process key figure)

◔ When

Phase closure Measure, continuously during the Analyze, Improve and Control Phases and after the completion of the project to secure sustainability

◎ Goal

Determine the process performance when no specification limits are set (focus on attaining target value).

▶▶ Steps

- Transform all values (x) into a new variable X:
  X = X current − X target.
- Calculate the interval range between X current and X target without considering outliers. A span (90) is usually used. The smaller the interval range the more effective the span.

$$\text{Span (90)} = X_{0.95} - X_{0.05}$$

- Optimize the process with the goal of attaining zero deviation (interval width = 0).

⇒ Tips

- The span is an excellent key figure for problems like delivery reliability.
- The percentiles can be calculated with programs like MS Excel®. With MS Excel® "QUANTIL (matrix, alpha)" is the syntax, whereby "matrix" stands for the whole data set, "alpha" for the percentile (e.g. 0.95).

An example of Span is given on the following page.

DEFINE

MEASURE

ANALYZE

IMPROVE

CONTROL

Example of Span

The new variable of X is the deviation (in days) between the agreed-to and the actual delivery date. The following data was collected for X:

X	$= \{-10, -9, -8, -7, -6, -5, -4, -3, -2, -1, 0, 1, 2, 3, 4, 5, 6, 7, 8, 9\}$
$X_{0.95}$	$= 8.05$
$X_{0.05}$	$= -9.05$
Span (90)	$= 8.05 - (-9.05) = 17.1$

C_p *and* C_{pk} *Values*

📁 **Terms**

C_p and C_{pk}

🕐 **When**

Phase closure Measure, continuously during Analyze and Improve, and in particular in the Control Phase

◎ **Goals**

– Identify the relationship between the customer specification limits (tolerance) and the natural range of the process (C_p value).
– Ascertain the centering of the process (C_{pk} value).

▶▶ **Steps**

C_p Value:

– Determine the upper and lower specification limits.
– Divide the distance between the upper and lower specification limits (tolerance) by six times the standard deviation of the process.
– If the data is not in normal distribution, divide the tolerance by the percentile range of ± 3 standard deviations (corresponds to 99.73 %).

With normal distribution	With non-normal distribution
$C_p = \dfrac{USL - LSL}{6s}$	$C_p = \dfrac{USL - LSL}{x_{0.99865} - x_{0.00135}}$

C_{pk} Value:

– Divide the distance between the nearest specification limit and the mean value by three times the standard deviation of the process. This also takes the location of the process into consideration.
– With non-normally distributed data: divide the distance between the nearest specification limit and the mean value by three times the standard deviation of the process.

With normal distribution	With non-normal distribution
$C_{pk} = \min\left[\dfrac{USL - \bar{x}}{3s} ; \dfrac{\bar{x} - LSL}{3s}\right]$	$C_{pk} = \min\left[\dfrac{USL - x_{0.5}}{x_{0.99865} - x_{0.5}} ; \dfrac{x_{0.5} - LSL}{x_{0.5} - x_{0.00135}}\right]$

DEFINE

MEASURE

ANALYZE

IMPROVE

CONTROL

DEFINE

MEASURE

ANALYZE

IMPROVE

CONTROL

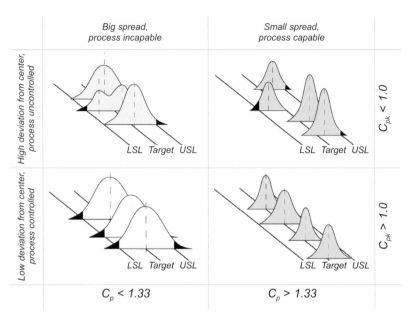

Tips

- A high C_p value is a necessary but not a sufficient condition for a good process Sigma value. A high process Sigma value can only be achieved when the process centering is taken into consideration, i.e. by a good C_{pk} value.
- To achieve a Sigma value of 6 (a Six Sigma process) the C_p and C_{pk} must assume the value of 2 (at least 6 standard deviations fit in between the mean and the customer specification limits). Due to the assumed process shifts of 1.5 standard deviations, Six Sigma[+Lean] corporations have set C_p values of 2 and C_{pk} values of 1.5 as their goal.
- If the observation is long term, the C_p and C_{pk} values are signified as P_p and P_{pk}.

Example of C_p and C_{pk} Values

For spray-painting operations, the specification limits are set as follows:
LSL = 100 and USL = 180. The collected data showed a mean value of 154.4
and a standard deviation of 22.86. The data is in normal distribution.

$$C_p = \frac{USL - LSL}{6s} = \frac{180 - 100}{6 \cdot 22.86} = 0.58$$

$$C_{pk} = min\left[\frac{USL - \bar{x}}{3s}; \frac{\bar{x} - LSL}{3s}\right] = min\left[\frac{180 - 154.54}{68.58}; \frac{154.54 - 100}{68.58}\right] = min\left[0.37; 0.79\right] = 0.37$$

Example: C_p and C_{pk} in Minitab®

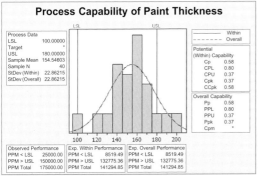

Process Capability of Paint Thickness

Process Data	
LSL	100.00000
Target	*
USL	180.00000
Sample Mean	154.54603
Sample N	40
StDev (Within)	22.86215
StDev (Overall)	22.86215

Within
Overall

Potential (Within) Capability	
Cp	0.58
CPL	0.80
CPU	0.37
Cpk	0.37
CCpk	0.58

Overall Capability	
Pp	0.58
PPL	0.80
PPU	0.37
Ppk	0.37
Cpm	*

Observed Performance		Exp. Within Performance		Exp. Overall Performance	
PPM < LSL	25000.00	PPM < LSL	8519.49	PPM < LSL	8519.49
PPM > USL	150000.00	PPM > USL	132775.36	PPM > USL	132775.36
PPM Total	175000.00	PPM Total	141294.85	PPM Total	141294.85

C_p = (USL - LSL) / (6s within) → >1 means: The process is narrower than the set limits.

CPU = (USL - m) / (3s within) → <1 means: The upper limit is exceeded.

CPL = (m - LSL) / (3s within) → <1 means: The lower limit is exceeded.

C_{pk} = min.{CPU, CPL} → <1 means: The process passes through both limits.

m = midpoint between USL, LSL

Graph result:
The upper and lower specification limits and a few statistical indicators from the sample:
The histogram shows how the data lies in relation with the specification limits. The curve depicts the normal distribution, taking into consideration the short and long-term observation. This example does not take this distinction into account.

The C_p and C_{pk} values: The greater the values the more capable the process.
C_p = 2 and C_{pk} = 1.5 matches a Six Sigma level.

The C_p and C_{pk} values: The greater the values the more capable the process.
C_p = 2 and C_{pk} = 1.5 matches a Six Sigma level.

DEFINE

MEASURE

ANALYZE

IMPROVE

CONTROL

DEFINE

MEASURE

ANALYZE

IMPROVE

CONTROL

Process Sigma

📁 **Term**
  Process Sigma, Sigma value

🕑 **When**
  Phase closure Measure, continuously during Analyze and Improve, and in particular in the Control Phase

◎ **Goals**
  – Depict the performance capability of a process, especially in relation to the specification limits.
  – Utilize as benchmark and/or best practice.

▶▶ **Steps**
  – Via **DPMO**
    Identify from the Sigma conversion table *(see appendix)*.

  – Via **Yield**
    Identify from the Sigma conversion table using first-pass yield.

  – Via **z-transformation**
    Identify solely with normally distributed, continuous data.

Z-method for Sigma Calculation
Prerequisite: continuous data in normal distribution

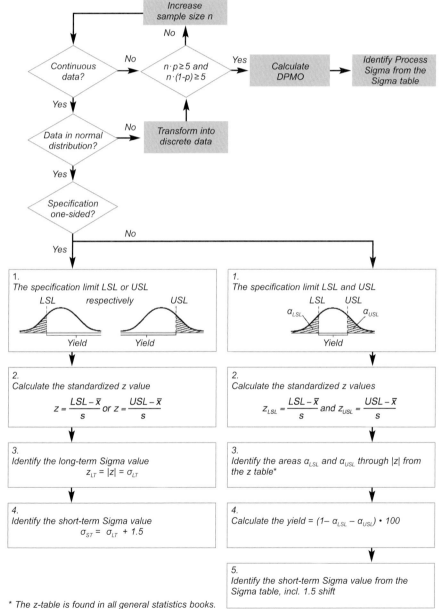

DEFINE

⇨ **Tip**

- Do not impose the Sigma value as the sole performance figure. Utilize those values and figures which customers and employees understand and accept.

MEASURE

Example of a Sigma Process Calculation
Example: two-sided CTQ

- Our customer asks for delivery seven days after placing the order at the earliest, but no later than twenty days. The standard deviation is four days.

- We thus have $z_{USL} = \dfrac{20 - 1.35}{4} = 1.625$ and $z_{LSL} = \dfrac{7 - 13.5}{4} = -1.625$

- From the z table* we obtain $\alpha_{USL} = 0.0516$ and $\alpha_{USL} = 0.0516$

- Yield = $(1 - 0.0516 - 0.0516) \cdot 100\% = 89.68\%$

- $\sigma_{ST} = 2.75$

- $\sigma_{LT} = 2.75 - 1.5 = 1.25$

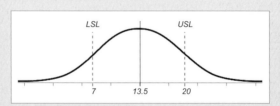

* *The z-table is found in all general statistics books.*

ANALYZE

IMPROVE

CONTROL

Checklist for the Measure Phase

Measurements
The most important output measurements are identified and
included in the operational definition. ☑

Every critical customer and business requirement is measurable
through (at least) one measurement. ☑

Data Collection
The data collection plan is drawn up. ☑

The necessary strategy for collecting data (scope and method)
is determined. ☑

Measurement System Analysis
The data quality is secured (e.g. through a Gage R & R). ☑

Evaluating Data
The data is depicted visually and interpreted. ☑

Performance Indicators
The current and relevant key performance indicators (DPMO, ppm,
DPU, Yield, C_p, C_{pk}, and Process Sigma) are calculated and
interpreted. ☑

Project Charter
The depiction of the problem and the project scope are reviewed
and adjusted if necessary. ☑

The expected net benefit is reviewed and adjusted if necessary. ☑

Measure
Carry out the Gate Review. ☑

DEFINE

MEASURE

ANALYZE

IMPROVE

CONTROL

DEFINE

MEASURE

ANALYZE

IMPROVE

CONTROL

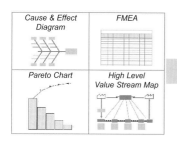

| Cause & Effect Diagram | FMEA |
| Pareto Chart | High Level Value Stream Map |

Tool 3: Input-Process Measurement Matrix

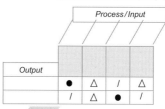

Process Analysis

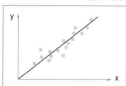

Passive Data Analysis

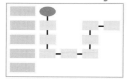

Active Data Analysis

No.	A	B	y
1	-	-	y1
2	+	-	y2
3	-	+	y3
4	+	+	y4

Analyze Closure

Suspected Root Cause	Verified through…	Main Causes	Potentials

DEFINE

MEASURE

ANALYZE

IMPROVE

CONTROL

Cause & Effect Diagram

☐ Terms
Cause & effect diagram, fishbone diagram, Ishikawa diagram

⊘ When
Analyze Phase, project selection, structuring of problem fields

◎ Goals
- Support the team in brainstorming possible causes.
- Visualize the possible causes.
- Depict the relation between possible causes.
- Focus the team on the possible causes for the problem (and not on symptoms).
- Create a shared understanding in the team for the underlying problem.

▶▶ Steps
- The specific problem is entered as the question "why" in a box on the right-hand side of the diagram ("fish head").
- The superordinated cause categories are entered as the first "fish bone". For this, the "6 Ms" have proven useful: Method, Man, Machine, Material, Measure, Mother Nature.
- Using brainstorming, focus on the causes for the problem formulated in the "fish head".
- Pursuing the "why" questions in more detail, identify the causes of the causes. Enter these into the diagram.
- All causes are then prioritized as follows:

  ⓒ = constant (the constant, invariable causes).

  ⓝ = noise (the causes which cannot be influenced directly and occur so to speak as "noise", e.g. lack of time).

  ⓧ = variable (the decisive variables which the project can influence).

⇨ **Tips**

- If the defined problem is complex it is advisable to draw up a cause & effect diagram per CTQ and CTB. Otherwise, the diagram can become too large and thus confusing.
- The more precise the question is in the "fish head", the better the result.
- Undertake a CNX evaluation from the viewpoint of the team: "What can be changed or influenced from the team's viewpoint?"
- To guarantee a clear overview, it is worthwhile to use different colors for different levels.
- The cause & effect diagram can be moderated in various ways: general brainstorming, analyzing the bones step by step, etc. The facilitator can select the best method for the situation.

Cause & Effect Diagram
Example: car dealer, spray-painting

Cause for the complaints after paintwork, main complaint: "Paint application is too thin."

Delays signing (April)
- Application too thin
- Rusts
- Paint flakes
- Wrong color
- Other
100%

Why is the paint application too thin?

Measures — No systematic measurement, Inaccurate
Mother Nature
Methods — Hit or miss settings, No guidelines
Man — Employee fluctuations, No incentives
Material
Machine — Obsolete machinery

FMEA

☐ Term

Failure mode and effect analysis (FMEA)

⊙ When

In the Analyze and Improve Phases, when selecting projects and prioritizing problematic areas

◎ Goals

– Identify causes and check for potential weak points.
– Specify priorities for the further analysis.
– Assess risks for the customer of a process.
– Deduce measures for reducing risk.

▶▶ Steps

Process / product: ①									FMEA Date: (Original)						
FMEA team:									(Revised)						
Black Belt:									Page:	of:					
FMEA process										Action results					
Position, function, process step	Potential failure mode	Potential effect(s) of failure	Severity	Potential cause(s) / mechanism(s) of failure	Frequency	Current control / regulating	Detection	RPN	Recommended action	Responsibility and target completion date	Action taken	Severity	Frequency	Detection	RPN
②	③	④	⑤	⑥	⑦	⑧	⑨⑩		⑪	⑫	⑬	⑭⑮⑯⑰			

① Note down general information about the project in the documentation sheet.

② Describe in detail the analyzed process or the analyzed product functions.

③ Characterize the potential failure opportunities: Why did the process / product fail to meet the requirements demanded by a specific operation?

④ Depict the effect of the failure opportunity / of the failure on the output.

5 Estimate the severity of the effect generated by the potential failure opportunity.

6 List the potential causes of the failure or the mechanisms triggering the failure.

7 Estimate the frequency with which the cause of the failure occurs during the performance of the process.

8 Specify the opportunities for identifying the failure cause or for avoiding its occurrence.

9 Estimate the probability of detecting a potential cause before the handover to the next process step.

10 Calculate the product of the severity, frequency, and detection probability. The rating result, known as the RPN (risk priority number), prioritizes the fields of action. If the RPN is high, a more detailed analysis is required.

11 Define the actions that reduce the frequency, severity, and / or the detection probability with the highest RPNs (Improve Phase).

12 Name the responsible persons and set the action's closing date.

13 Describe the measures actually taken and state the implementation date.

14 Estimate the effect of a potential failure opportunity on the customer after the improvement measure has been implemented.

15 Estimate the frequency with which the failure cause occurs during the execution of the process after the improvement has been implemented.

16 Estimate the probability of detecting a potential cause before the handover to the next process step after the improvement has been implemented.

17 Recalculate the RPN.

DEFINE

MEASURE

ANALYZE

IMPROVE

CONTROL

Rating Scale: Severity	
1	Remains unnoticed and has no effect on performance
2	Remains unnoticed and has only a minor effect on performance
3	Causes only minor inconveniences
4	Causes a minor loss of performance
5	Causes a loss of performance which results in a customer complaint
6	Causes a loss of performance which results in partial malfunction
7	Causes a malfunction which results in customer dissatisfaction
8	Product or service is unusable
9	Product or service is illegal
10	Customer or employee could be injured or killed

Rating Scale: Frequency	
1	Once every 100 years
2	Once every 5-100 years
3	Once every 3-5 years
4	Once every 1-3 years
5	Once per year
6	Once every 6 months
7	Once per month
8	Once per week
9	Once per day
10	Several times per day

DEFINE

MEASURE

ANALYZE

IMPROVE

CONTROL

DEFINE

MEASURE

ANALYZE

IMPROVE

CONTROL

	Rating Scale: Detection Probability
1	Cause of the defect is obvious and can easily be prevented
2	All units are inspected automatically
3	Statistic process control with systematic inspection of failure causes and prevention measures
4	Statistic process control is carried out with systematic inspection of failure causes
5	Statistic process control is carried out
6	All units are checked manually and prevention measures are installed
7	All units are checked manually
8	Frequent manual inspection of failure causes
9	Occasional manual inspection of failure causes
10	The failure caused is not detectable

⇨ **Tips**
- There is a need for action if the RPN is > 125. If the rating for one of the three evaluations (severity, frequency, detection probability) is = 10, then even when the overall RPN < 125 the process / product needs to be checked in detail to see if there is need for action.
- Visualize the criteria for estimating severity, frequency, and detection probability so that everyone understands – this prevents unnecessary discussions.
- The evaluation criteria can be adjusted to suit the company.

Example FMEA
Example: car dealer

Process / product: Color mixing							FMEA Date: (Original)								
FMEA team: Mr. Jones, Mr. Rubble, Mr. Smith							(Revised)								
Black Belt: Mr. Lincoln							Page: 1	of: 2							
FMEA process									Action results						
Position, function, process step	Potential failure mode	Potential effect(s) of failure	Severity	Potential cause(s) / mechanism(s) of failure	Frequency	Current control / regulating	Detection	RPN	Recommended action	Responsibility and target completion date	Action taken	Severity	Frequency	Detection	RPN
Color mixing	Wrong color	Color wrong	8	Incorrect on shelf	5	None	9	360							
	Wrong job	Color wrong	8	Wrongly filed away	4	None	9	288							
	Wrong setting	Color wrong	8	No training	9	None	9	648							

DEFINE

MEASURE

ANALYZE

IMPROVE

CONTROL

Process Flow Chart

☐ **Term**
Flow chart

🕓 **When**
In the Analyze (current process), Improve, and Control Phases (should-be process)

◎ **Goals**
– Simplify understanding by providing a visual depiction of the process: "A picture says more than a 1000 words."
– Create a shared understanding amongst the team for the problem.
– Clarify the individual process steps.
– Identify the process structure.
– Establish the basis for advanced process analysis.
– Identify the potentials for optimization and improvement in the processes.
– Clarify the complexity.

▶▶ **Steps**
– Depict all functions, which are involved in the process flow.
– Accentuate the starting and endpoints, oriented on a high-level mapping, e.g. SIPOC.
– Identify the process steps through brainstorming before drawing up the actual chart. Every step is made up of a noun and verb (e.g.: "gather job documentation", "check credit details").
– Plot all the identified steps in their actual, correct sequence in the flow. Use standardized symbols for this purpose.

DEFINE

MEASURE

ANALYZE

IMPROVE

CONTROL

Symbols

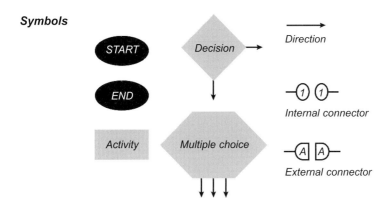

Internal connector: within one page
External connector: between different sides

⇨ **Tip**

For the decision, prefer to direct the "No" branch to the right, the "Yes" branch downwards. Structuring the chart in this way helps to avoid confusion.

Example of a Process Flow Chart

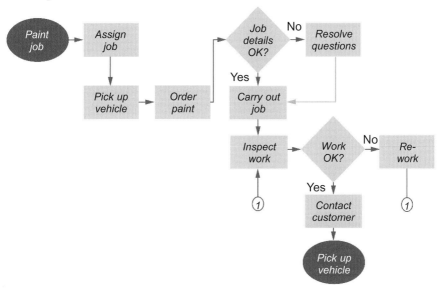

DEFINE

MEASURE

ANALYZE

IMPROVE

CONTROL

Cross-Functional Diagram

🗀 **Terms**

Cross-functional diagram, swim-lane diagram

🕐 **When**

In the Analyze, Improve, and Control Phases

◎ **Goal**

Assign the individual steps in a process to the corresponding responsible functions (persons / departments).

▶▶ **Steps**

1. Identify the persons involved in the process, write their functions on cards, and organize these cards vertically.
2. Describe the action that triggers the process. Write this on a card and place it next to the card with the respective function.
3. Repeat this for the final step in the process and position the card at the end of the diagram.
4. Describe the other activities and assign them to their matching function in chronological order.

⇨ **Tip**

In the Improve Phase (should-be process) always depict the process first and then the functions. Follow the rule "Organizational structure follows the operational structure."

Example of a Cross-Functional Diagram
Example: car dealer, paint workshop

Customer	Paint job
Customer service	
Workshop foreman	Assign job
Operator	Pick up vehicle
Body work	
Storage	Order paint

Resolve questions — No

Inspect work — Work OK? — Yes — Contact customer — Pick up vehicle

Job details OK? — Yes — Carry out job

No — Re-work

DEFINE

MEASURE

ANALYZE

IMPROVE

CONTROL

Interface Analysis

⬚ **Term**
Interface Analysis

🕐 **When**
In the Analyze Phase

◎ **Goal**
Identify and analyze interfaces. These are the points within the process where responsibility is handed over to another function. As a rule, this interface means that work stops or is delayed. They are usually very prone to errors.

▶▶ **Step**
Search for gaps, unnecessary and unclear requirements, complicated handovers, incompatible goals, and common problem areas. The analysis helps to gain deeper insights into the causes having an effect on quality problems.

⇢ **Tip**
Frequent returns to a function (loops) only make sense when they are really necessary (e.g. important reviews / releases). Loops have to be scrutinized closely to make sure they are justifiable.

Example of an Interface Analysis
Example: car dealer, paint workshop

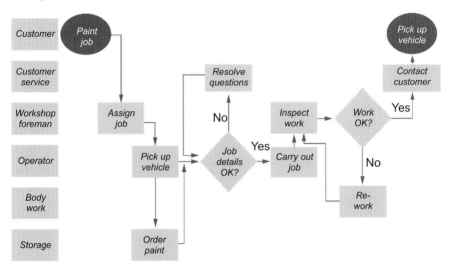

Are so many interfaces necessary?

Could it make more sense to have the paint readily available in small storage or directly in the workshop?

DEFINE

MEASURE

ANALYZE

IMPROVE

CONTROL

Spaghetti Diagram

📁 **Term**
Spaghetti Diagram

🕐 **When**
In the Analyze and Improve Phase

◎ **Goals**
- Identify suboptimal transport and motion in the current process (Analyze Phase).
- Optimize the shopfloor-layout in order to minimize these non-value-adding activities in the should-be process (Improve Phase).

▶▶ **Step**
- Display shopfloor-layout.
- Draw lines representing all distances covered between different steps.
- Highlight areas / ways that are critical/suboptimal.

⇨ **Tip**
- Use differently coloured lines for different persons.
- Include also machines (e.g. fork lift) in the picture in order to identify areas with high accident risk.

Example of a Spaghetti Diagram

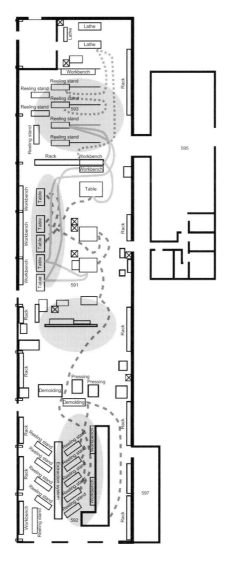

Value Analysis

🗀 **Term**

Value analysis

🕐 **When**

In the Analyze Phase

◎ **Goal**

Identify the value-adding, value-enabling, and non-value-adding activities in a process. Optimizing a process means maximizing the proportion of value-adding activities, while eliminating non-value-adding activities as far as possible or at least reducing them to a minimum.

What are value-adding, value-enabling, and non-value-adding activities?

– **Value-adding activities:**
These are activities which add value to a product or service from the customer's point of view when they are first carried out. They are ultimately the sole source for ensuring that customer requirements are met fully and profitably. It is of fundamental importance to increase the proportion of value-adding activities.

– **Non-value-adding activities:**
These activities are indispensable due to insufficient preconditions. A customer would never regard them as essential and would never be willing to pay for them. These activities are to be eliminated or reduced to a minimum when optimizing the process.

– **Value-enabling activities:**
These activities are not value-adding as such. They are necessary for providing the product or service, or at the least for facilitating performance. A reduction of these activities to a specific degree is required by the organization.

▶▶ **Step**

Characterize every activity in the process map as value-adding, value-enabling, or non-value-adding.

⇢ **Tips**

- The root competence of a company must be obvious in order to judge what is value-adding and non-value-adding. For a transport company, the key value-adding activity is to provide transport services to and from the customer; for a manufacturer, transport is not value-adding for a product or service.
- It has proven worthwhile to mark the cards representing the process steps in different colors (with adhesive dots or colored pen): red = non-value-adding activities, green = value-adding activities and blue = value-enabling activities.
- Do not waste time discussing whether an activity is "red" or "blue". When in doubt, mark the activity red. The need to discuss is a clear sign that this activity possesses optimizing potential.

The Seven Types of Waste

In the 1970s Taiichi Ohno, father of the Toyota production system, defined the seven types of waste (acronym: TIMWOOD)

1	T	ransport (movement of materials / products from one place to another)
2	I	ventory (materials / products wait for processing)
3	M	otion (surplus of movement or poor ergonomics)
4	W	aiting (delay caused by constraints, releases, idle times)
5	O	verproduction (more is produced than needed)
6	O	ver-processing, over-development (more value added than the customer is willing to pay for, waste in the process)
7	D	efects / rework (correcting errors)

The Seven Office Sins are presented on the following page.

The Seven Office Sins
Sources of waste in service industries

1	*Unnecessary information transport*	– Superfluous movement of documents from workplace to workplace, between administrative and production – Passing through authorization chains, hierarchies and filing procedures which are unnecessary
2	*Unnecessary stock*	Storing of completed projects, unused working materials and data, multiple filing
3	*Unnecessary movement*	– Employees have to move around to search for documents and/or colleagues who work elsewhere – Ergonomic hindrances
4	*Waiting times, idle times, search times*	Waiting for releases and/or decisions by superiors, return of files, passing on of assignments, warm-times of office equipment, suboptimal network filing
5	*Information overflow*	More information as necessary, e.g. e-mails, copies, memos, etc.
6	*Useless activities*	Compiling of reports, statistics and protocols nobody reads. Repeated manually entering of data, unnecessary copying
7	*Defects*	Media breaks in the data formats, illegible faxes and notes, incomplete specifications

Time Analysis

📁 **Term**

Time analysis

🕐 **When**

In the Analyze Phase

◎ **Goals**

- Analyze the recorded times.
- Gain a better understanding of the process.
- Clarify the effect of process steps without value added on the time that is necessary for producing a product or the provision of a service.
- Identify constraints in the process.
- In connection with the value analysis, identify approaches for implementing change or improvement.
- Create a basis for quantifying the opportunities at the end of the Analyze Phase.

▶▶ **Steps**

- Record or estimate times which deliver knowledge that is more detailed about the causes or drivers of the basic problem. *Examples:* Setup times, idle times, transport times, and route times, etc.
- Structure the recording of these times around each process step or summarize them over many steps (added-up times).

⇢ **Tips**

- Time data must not exist for all process activities.
- Possible sources:
  - Activity reports, shift logbooks, diaries, activity and note books,
  - Calendars, day planners, and telephone messages,
  - Files, studies, and reports,
  - Computer time recordings.
- If no data is available: Estimate times at first and then measure them in the next step.

DEFINE

MEASURE

ANALYZE

IMPROVE

CONTROL

- Make use of at least five data points to calculate the mean time.
- It is usually sufficient to record only the overall lead time and the processing times. The idle times result from the difference.

Example of a Time Analysis

Example: cross-functional process diagram with time analysis/car dealer, spray-painting workshop

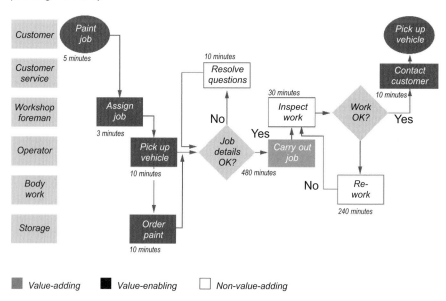

144

Value Stream Map

🗀 **Term**

Value stream map

🕐 **When**

In the Analyze and Improve Phases

◎ **Goals**

- Identify the material and information flow of a product or a product group from "ramp to ramp".
- Identify sources of waste and their causes.
- Reduce lead time.
- Generate a comprehensive overview of the process; this enables us to avoid "local sub-optimizations" that take place due to the limited focus on sub-areas.
- Create a basis for implementing new product systems.
- Derive priorities on the basis of process-related data and the description of activities, so as to influence these values in the future.

▶▶ **Steps**

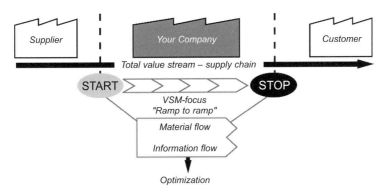

- The variants for drawing up a value stream map on a different level can be classified as follows into the DMAIC cycle:

DEFINE

MEASURE

ANALYZE

IMPROVE

CONTROL

145

- Define: SIPOC
- Analyze: From the high-level to the low-level value stream map – "Current-State-VSM"
- Improve: Should-be value stream map – "Future-State-VSM"

Stage model for drawing up a value stream map

1. *Define process and products:*
   Generate an overview of all relevant process information on a high level using a SIPOC Diagram.
   Define the process frame by marking the start and stop events.

   Document the current state with the help of a top-down process diagram: Subdivide the core process vertically into individual sub-processes. Then identify the right level of observation for drawing up the value stream.

   Identify the customer-relevant product groups or families in order to focus on the areas in the value stream map, which have the greatest impact on the customer (ABC / XYZ analysis).

2. *Draw a process diagram:*
   Draw the entire value strea. The direction of observation should move from dispatch "upstream".

Process step   *Customer / supplier*   *Transport*

Product to customer

300 parts
7 days
Inventory

3. *Define the material and information flow:*
   Distinguish the directions in which the material flows in the process be-tween push and pull movements. Include all inspections of goods re-ceived and quality checks.

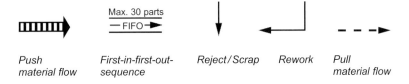

| Push material flow | First-in-first-out-sequence | Reject/Scrap | Rework | Pull material flow |

Then document the flow direction of the information, from incoming orders to release for production (type and frequency of customer orders, produc-tion releases, procuring orders).

Electronic information:
type, frequency, and method

Manual information:
type, frequency, and method

4. *Define the process data boxes and times:*
   Document all process-relevant data (processing time, setup time, reject/scrap rate, yield, machine availability, etc).

   Define the process-related lead times and proportional, value-adding and non-value-adding times. Derive the indicators for determining process efficiency.

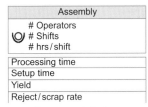

Process data box

5. *Validate the current state:*
   Have those involved in the process checked the drawn up value stream map in order to validate all interfaces, material, and information flows?

⇒ Tips

- Verify the correctness of the pull movements in the value stream map.
- Ensure that all rework steps are noted.
- Verify the measurements noted in the data boxes.
- ***Important:*** Pay attention to units in the calculation – takt rates or daily exit rates etc. are to be converted into either hours or minutes.

Example Value Stream Map

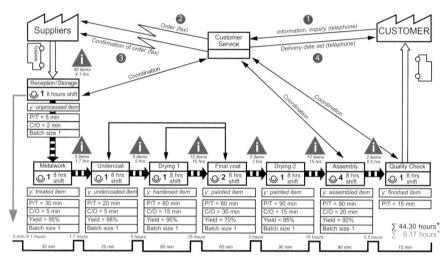

* *Non-value-adding*
* *Value-adding*

The Importance of Speed

📁 **Terms**
Little's law, process efficiency (PE)

🕐 **When**
In the Analyze Phase

◎ **Goals**
- Describe the connection between WIP ("work in process") and the exit rate as well as its impact on the process lead time (Little's law).
- Identify sources of waste such as setup times, idle times, waiting times, scrap and rework, which are hidden by high WIP inventories.
- Reduce the process lead time by reducing inventory and raising capacity at the "constraint".
- Create a best-practice benchmark based on the process efficiency as the percentage proportion of the whole process lead time in which the product is improved or an added value is created from the customer's point of view.

▶▶ **Steps**
Basic definitions:
- **Exit rate**
  The maximum product quantity (output) that a process produces within a specific time period.

- **Bottleneck**
  The process step that causes the greatest time delays in a process – there can only be one bottleneck in a process!

- **Constraint**
  A process characterized as a bottleneck that is not capable of producing the exit rate (internal or external) demanded by the customer.
  Production is below the takt rate geared to customer needs.
  A constraint is always a bottleneck, but a bottleneck must not always be a constraint!

DEFINE

MEASURE

ANALYZE

IMPROVE

CONTROL

Determine the process lead time using Little's law:
- **Process Lead Time** (PLT) [time]:
  The time between a product entering the production process and its completion.

- **Work in Process** (WIP) [quantity]:
  Inventories within the process, each complete work operation that has been started but not yet ended. A "work operation" can, for example, occur through materials, assignments, orders, waiting customers, assembling work, e-mails, etc.

- **Exit Rate** [quantity / time]:
  The output of a process within a specific time.

Little's Law

$$PLT = \frac{WIP}{exit\ rate}\ [time]$$

PLT   = process lead time [time]
WIP   = work in process [quantity]
Exit rate = process output [quantity / time]

min. PLT ↓

$$\frac{min.\ WIP \downarrow}{max.\ exit\ rate \uparrow}$$

Determine the process efficiency:
- **Value-Adding Time**:
  Time in which the product is "improved" and value is added to the product. The customer is willing to pay for this.

$$Process\ efficiency = \frac{value\text{-}adding\ time\ [t]}{process\ lead\ time\ [t]} \cdot 100$$

⇨ **Tips**
- "Traditional" process improvements aim exclusively at increasing the exit rate if the process lead time is to be reduced. This approach brings with it higher costs, e.g. demands greater investments, longer working hours and more stock. Excellent process improvements optimize first of all the processes with the aim of stabilizing and then reducing the WIP (generic pull system, reducing non-value-adding time). The exit rate should first

be addressed when all other improvement methods (setup time reduction, reducing idle times, etc) have been applied and constraints still
exist.

- Processes with low Process Efficiency are sources of enormous potential for reducing costs.
- The majority of company processes have a Process Efficiency of less
than 10 %. They are frequently characterized by high inventory levels,
a fact that in turn impacts negatively on the overall process lead time
and reaction capability.

Typical and World-Class Cycle Efficiencies

Application	Typical Cycle Efficiency	World-class Cycle Efficiency
Machining	1 %	20 %
Fabrication	10 %	25 %
Assembly	15 %	35 %
Continuous manufacturing	30 %	80 %
Business processes - transactional	10 %	50 %
Business processes - creative / cognitive	5 %	25 %

Source: Lean Six Sigma, Michael George, 2002, p. 37.

Identifying Process Constraints

📁 **Terms**
Process constraint identification, process balancing

🕐 **When**
In the Analyze Phase

◎ **Goals**
- Identify the bottlenecks in the process determining capacity, causing long lead times, high inventories of finished goods, and high inventories of unfinished products or WIP.
- Identify those constraints in the process which hinder the quantity demanded by the customer from being produced.

▶▶ **Steps**

Step 1
Collect the necessary data
Determine the entire customer demand, the available net time and the net capacity per process step.

Step 2
Calculate the takt rate (customer demand) or takt time
- *Takt rate* [quantity / time]:
  The quantity of a product (output) demanded by a customer over a continuous period of time.

$$\text{Takt rate} = \frac{\text{no. of units to be produced (acc. to customer demand)}}{\text{available production time}}$$

- *Takt time* [time / quantity]:
  The takt time describes the time span in which a specific process step / sub-process has to be completed if the product is to be delivered in line with customer requirements at the end of the overall process.

$$\text{Takt time} = \frac{\text{available production time}}{\text{no. of units to be produced (acc. to customer demand)}}$$

Step 3

Analyze the figures

Relate the processing times or exit rates of the observed process steps to the calculated takt rate or takt time by using a chart.

– The process step with the lowest exit rates represents the most time-consuming operation, a bottleneck.
– If this bottleneck does not meet the takt rate (customer demands), this is a constraint.

Exit rate (quantity/time)

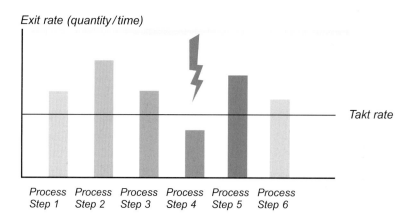

Takt rate

Process   Process   Process   Process   Process   Process
Step 1   Step 2   Step 3   Step 4   Step 5   Step 6

Tool 3: Input-Process Measurement Matrix

📁 **Terms**

Tool 3: Input-Process Measurement matrix, output measurement matrix

🕙 **When**

In the Analyze Phase

◎ **Goals**

- Identify and measure the key influencing variables (input and process measurements).
- Depict their relation to the output measurements.

▶▶ **Steps**

- Enter the output measurements identified and selected in tool 2 into a matrix.
- Compare the process and input variables from the cause&effect diagram as well as sensibly derived measurement categories.
- Mark the suspected relationships between output, process, and input measurements in the matrix. These suspected relationships will be verified later using statistical methods.

⇒ **Tips**

- When undertaking an effectiveness-driven project, examine only the influencing variables as to the relationship between effectiveness/quality in tool 3.
- When undertaking efficiency-driven projects, the influencing variables should be examined as to the relationship between efficiency/costs.

Example of Tool 3: Input-Process Measurement Matrix
Example: cause-related measurements

Output measurements	Work flows Processing time per job	Undercoat Under-coat thickness	Spray-painting Thickness of basic application	Final varnishing Thickness of varnish	Paint/varnish-mix Amount of thinner	Process-/ input-variables Input-/process-measurement
Paint thickness in micrometers	△	●	●	●	○	
Sags, drips, etc.	△	●	●	●	○	
Coloration	/	/	○	○	●	
Deviation current/target for customer handover	○	/	/	/	/	

● *Strong relationship* ○ *Moderate relationship* △ *Weak relationship* / *No relationship*

DEFINE

MEASURE

ANALYZE

IMPROVE

CONTROL

155

Data Stratification

□ **Term**
Stratification

🕑 **When**
In the Analyze Phase

◎ **Goals**
– Break up the data from different distributions or populations, e.g. when the histogram has several peaks.
– Break down data to recognize new structures with which we can limit and explain a problem, e.g. when a problem occurs at different times, at different places, or under different conditions.

▶▶ **Steps**
– Group data into meaningful categories (key characteristics), for example:
  - Who: Persons, departments, suppliers.
  - What: Machines, equipment, products, services.
  - Where: Locations, regions.
  - When: Weekdays, seasons.

– Depict and analyze the stratified data in graphs. If no relationships are evident, this can mean that:
  - The causes are not yet correctly identified. Stratify the data further or contrast it in a graph with data stratified in another way.
  - All possible causes have the same effect on the process. Eliminate the causes one after the other. Here: No result is also a result!

Example of Data Stratification

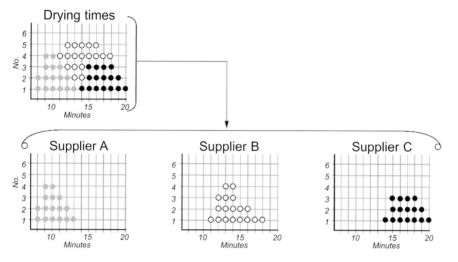

DEFINE

MEASURE

ANALYZE

IMPROVE

CONTROL

DEFINE

MEASURE

ANALYZE

IMPROVE

CONTROL

Transforming Data

🗀 **Term**
Transforming data

🕙 **When**
In the Measure, Analyze, Control Phases

◎ **Goal**
Transform data of any distribution into data in normal distribution. A number of statistical methods assume normally distributed data. If this assumption is not met, the generated statistical results are less reliable.

▶▶ **Steps**
1. Ensure that the data stems from one population (see data stratification).

2. Identify the necessary transformation function. There are different methods for transforming data:
    -   Linear transformations of the form $ax + b$. As a rule, these do not change the distribution of the data.
    -   Non-linear transformations are frequently able to align the data to that of a normal distribution. The usual non-linear transformation functions are:

Logarithms	$\log x, \ln x$
Exponential	$\exp x$
Logit	$\ln = \left(\dfrac{x}{1-x} \right)$
Reciprocal	$\dfrac{1}{x}$
Square	x^2
Square root	$\sqrt{x}$
Root	$\sqrt[n]{x}$
Box-Cox	x^λ

The Box Cox transformation is supported automatically by numerous statistical programs like Minitab®. Here the transformation parameter λ (lambda) is estimated simultaneously with the other model parameters (e.g. mean value). Depending on the estimated λ value, the Box Cox transformation can correspond to one of the usual transformation functions (e.g. $\lambda = 2$ corresponds to x^2).

Which transformation functions are to be used?
-   If the physical relationship is known we can select a transformation that can be easily interpreted. If for example, the relationship arises multiplicatively, the data becomes additive through logarithms (ln x).
-   In practice however, we have to work on a trail-and-error basis because the relationship is usually unknown.

3. Test the data for normal distribution to see if the transformation has fulfilled its purpose.

⇨ **Tip**

It is often better to seek statistical methods that are robust against data not normally distributed. The disadvantage of transformation is that it is often difficult to interpret transformed data.

DEFINE

MEASURE

ANALYZE

IMPROVE

CONTROL

Example of Data Transformation
Example: Box Cox transformation

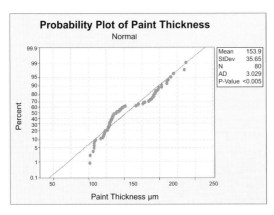

Result:
the histograms showing paint thickness structured according to locations (see data stratification) indicate that the data of branch 1 are normally distributed. This assumption is to be tested.

If the p-value is greater than 0.05, we can assume that there is normal distribution. Here the p-value is smaller than 0.05, meaning that we can reject the null hypothesis of normal distribution.

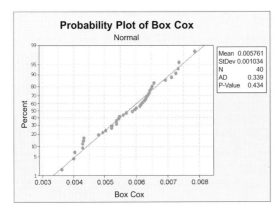

Result:
test the transformed data for normality. Because p is > 0.05, we can assume that the transformed data is normally distributed.

160

Hypothesis Testing

📁 **Terms**

Hypothesis testing, statistical tests

🕑 **When**

In the Analyze and Control Phases

◎ **Goals**

- Make it easier to decide on the validity of the assumptions made, e. g. concerning the parameters of a population.
- Verify the suspected causes.
- Ascertain statistical differences between two or more process outputs.
- Ascertain statistically significant improvements after their implementation.

▶▶ **Steps**

A statistical test is a procedure that verifies the statistical significance of a hypothesis for a sample using a test statistic. Statistical tests are also called hypothesis or significance tests.

Every statistical test involves the formulation of two complimentary assertions: The null hypothesis and the alternative hypothesis:

- **The null hypothesis (H_0)**
  describes the supposition that a test parameter *equals* a given value or that the parameters of two or more populations are equal. Thus, as a rule the null hypothesis describes the status quo, the state in which nothing has changed (condition of equality), or a specific state (e.g. data follow the normal distribution).

- **The alternative hypothesis (H_A)**
  on the other hand describes the supposition that a tested parameter is *unequal* to a given value or that the comparison of different parameters will show that at least one of these is different. The alternative hypothesis represents the change.

Statistical tests can only ascertain differences, not compliances. For this reason, as a rule the null hypothesis is established in order to be rejected.

The purpose of the alternative hypothesis – also known as the working hypothesis – is to reject the null hypothesis as inapplicable.

Making decisions based on a statistical test entails a certain degree of uncertainty: one cannot be 100 % certain that the decision is correct. At the same time however, statistical tests are designed in such a way that the probability of making an incorrect decision is minimized. A null hypothesis is rejected when the calculation result using the sample leads to the conclusion that it (the established null hypothesis) is very unlikely. What is ultimately considered to be improbable is determined in advance by the so-called significance level. The most frequently used significance levels are 0.05 (= 5 %) or 0.01 (= 1 %). The significance level is connected with the potential wrong decision.

There are two types of wrong decisions or error types in statistical tests: the α-error and the β-error.

		Reality	
		H_0	H_A
Decision	H_0	Correct decision	β-error (error of 2nd type)
	H_A	α-error (error of 1st type)	Correct decision

Example: Trial hearing

H_0	The accused is innocent.
H_A	The accused is guilty.
α-error	The accused is found guilty when in fact he is innocent.
β-error	The accused is acquitted when he is in fact guilty.

For a statistical test both α and β should be kept as small as possible (usually α = 0.05 and β = 0.10). However: The smaller the α-value the larger β becomes.
The α-value is determined prior to the test and sets the maximum risk that the tester is prepared to take of making an error of the 1st type.

The p-value, linked with the result of every statistical test, is calculated from the test statistic on the basis of existing data and sets the empirical probability for an error of the 1st type. If the calculated p-value is smaller than the α-value, the null hypothesis can be rejected because the empirical error probability is smaller than what the tester has maximally allowed.

The p-value thus corresponds to the remaining risk when rejecting the null hypothesis that the null hypothesis is right after all.
Example: With α = 0.05 the null hypothesis is rejected when p is = 0.04. There remains a residual risk of 4 % that the null hypothesis is right after all.

The following steps occur in a statistical test:
1. Define the problem and goal (what is being investigated for which purpose?).
2. Formulate the hypothesis (H_0: condition of equality).
3. Set the significance level α (as a rule α = 0.05 or α = 0.01).
4. Select a suitable statistical test (e.g. Two Sample-t-Test).
5. Carry out the test statistic with the aid of a statistical software (e.g. Minitab®).
6. Interpret the test statistic or p-value.
7. Make your decision.
8. Verify your decision. If H_0 is not rejected, then verify β!

There are a great number of statistical tests. The most relevant tests for the project work are described on the following pages.

DEFINE

MEASURE

ANALYZE

IMPROVE

CONTROL

Discrete data – testing proportions

Test	When/What for	Hypotheses	Prerequisites
Binomial test One-Proportion test	Compare the proportion of a characteristic of a population with a given target proportion	$H_0 : p = p_{Target}$ $H_A : p \neq p_{Target}$	Binominally distributed data $n \geq 100$ and $n \cdot p \geq 5$ and $n \cdot (1-p) \geq 5$
Binomial test Two-Proportion test	Compare proportions of a characteristic from two populations	$H_0 : p_1 = p_2$ $H_A : p_1 \neq p_2$	Binominally distributed data $n \geq 100$ and $n \cdot p \geq 5$ and $n \cdot (1-p) \geq 5$
χ^2 Homogeneity test Chi-Square test	Compare proportions in two or more populations	$H_0 : p_1^1 = p_1^2 = \ldots = p_1^j$ $p_2^1 = p_2^2 = \ldots = p_2^j$ $\vdots$ $p_j^1 = p_j^2 = \ldots = p_j^j$ $H_A :$ *At least one proportion is different*	Nominal data $n \geq 100$ and expected value for each cell $X_{ij}^e > 5$

Continuous data – testing mean values

Test	When/what for	Hypotheses	Prerequisites
One-sample t-test	Compare the mean value of a population with a target value	$H_0: \mu = \mu_{Target}$ $H_A: \mu \neq \mu_{Target}$	n $\geq$ 30 or normally distributed data
Two-sample t-test	Compare mean values of two independent populations	$H_0: \mu_1 = \mu_2$ $H_A: \mu_1 \neq \mu_2$	n $\geq$ 30 or normally distributed data, independent samples
Two-sample paired t-test	Compare mean values of two paired populations	$H_0: \mu_1 = \mu_2$ $H_A: \mu_1 \neq \mu_2$	n $\geq$ 30 or normally distributed data, paired dependent samples
One-way ANOVA	Compare mean values of several independent populations	$H_0: \mu_1 = \mu_2 = \ldots = \mu_i$ $H_A:$ *At least one mean value is different*	Equal variances or equal sample sizes, independent samples

DEFINE

MEASURE

ANALYZE

IMPROVE

CONTROL

DEFINE

MEASURE

ANALYZE

IMPROVE

CONTROL

Continuous data – testing variance

Test	When/what for	Hypotheses	Prerequisites
One-sample χ^2-test	Compare variance of one population with a target value	$H_0 : \sigma^2 = \sigma^2_{Target}$ $H_A : \sigma^2 \neq \sigma^2_{Target}$	Normally distributed data
Two-sample F-test or Levene's test Two variances	Compare the variances of two independent populations	$H_0 : \sigma_1^2 = \sigma_2^2$ $H_A : \sigma_1^2 \neq \sigma_2^2$	F-test: normally distributed data. Levene's test: no distribution assumption, independent samples
ANOVA – test for equal variances (Bartlett's and Levene's test)	Compare variances of several independent populations	$H_0 : \sigma_1^2 = \sigma_2^2 = \ldots = \sigma_i^2$ H_A: At least one variance is different.	Bartlett's test: normally distributed data. Levene's test: no distribution assumption, independent samples

Example of a One-Sample t-Test

Result:

```
One-Sample T: Paint thickness

Test of mu = 140 vs not = 140


Variable      N     Mean    StDev   SE Mean              95% CI      T     P
Paint
thickness    80  153.859   35.654    3.986  (145.925; 161.793)  3.48  0.001
```

Here p is < 0.05. There exists a statistically significant difference. The hypothesis H_0 can be rejected.

Example of a One-Sample t-Test

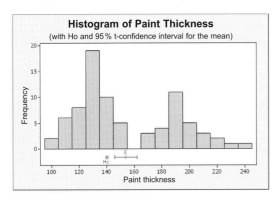

Graph result:
the difference between the target and mean values of the sample is statistically significant.
The hypothesis H_0 of $\mu = 140$ can be rejected.

DEFINE

MEASURE

ANALYZE

IMPROVE

CONTROL

One-Factorial ANOVA

▢ **Terms**
ANOVA, Analysis of Variances, one-factorial variance analysis, one-way ANOVA

◷ **When**
In the Analyze Phase

◎ **Goal**
Examine the relationship of a discrete, independent variable on a continuous, dependent output.

▶▶ **Steps**
The independent variables are characterized as factors, the single expressions of these factors as factor levels. The two types of variance analysis are distinguished according to the number of factors:
One factor: One-factorial variance analysis (one-way ANOVA)
Two factors: Two-factorial variance analysis (two-way ANOVA)

Using a test statistic, ANOVA identifies if the variability between the groups (factor levels) is larger than the variability within the group (factor level). In this case, differences exist between the groups.
The whole variation is broken down. In ANOVA this breakdown can be transferred to the sum of the deviations of all observations.

Total deviation = explained deviation + non-explained deviation

Sum of the squared total deviation

*Sum of the squared deviation **between** the factor levels*

*Sum of the squared deviation **within** the factor level*

$$\sum_{i=1}^{a}\sum_{j=1}^{n}(y_{ij}-\bar{y})^2 = n\cdot\sum_{i=1}^{a}(\bar{y}_i-\bar{y})^2 + \sum_{i=1}^{a}\sum_{j=1}^{n}(y_{ij}-\bar{y}_i)^2$$

$$SS_{Total} = SS_{Factor\ levels} + SS_{Error}$$

The division of the addition of the squares by the corresponding number of degrees of freedom enables us to make a good estimate of the average spread within and between the factor levels:

$$MS_{Total} = \left(\frac{SS_{Total}}{a \cdot n - 1} \right)$$

$$MS_{Factor\ levels} = \left(\frac{SS_{Factor\ levels}}{a - 1} \right)$$

$$MS_{Error} = \left(\frac{SS_{Error}}{a(n - 1)} \right)$$

The values $MS_{Factor\ levels}$ and MS_{Error} are set in relationship to one another. This expression is formed by the test statistic for the ANOVA test of same mean values.

$$F = \frac{MS_{Factor\ levels}}{MS_{Error}}$$

The larger the average spread between the factor levels is in comparison to the average spread within the factor level, the greater the test statistic (F-value) and the more probable it becomes that a significant difference exists between the mean values.

$$y_{ij} = \mu + \tau_i + \varepsilon_{ij}$$

ij-observation   *Random error*

Total mean value

Effect of the i-th factor level

The null hypothesis is: H_0: $\mu_1 = \mu_2 = \dots = \mu_l$
and accordingly the alternative hypothesis: H_A: $\mu_i \neq \mu_j$ for at least one pair (i, j).

The hypotheses could be alternatively formulated as: H_0: $\tau_1 = \tau_2 = \dots = \tau_l = 0$
or: H_A: $\tau_i \neq 0$ for at least one i.

Example of One-Factorial Variance Analysis

The suspected cause – that the results achieved by four operators (factor levels of the factor "operator") are different – is to be verified.

```
One-way ANOVA: Paint thickness versus Operator

Source        DF      SS      MS      F      P
Operator       3   19853    6618   6.24  0.001
Error         76   80571    1060
Total         79  100424

S = 32.56    R-Sq = 19.77%   R-Sq(adj) = 16.60%

                             Individual 95% CIs For Mean Based on
                             Pooled StDev
Level    N    Mean   StDev  ---+---------+---------+---------+------
AH      20  129.23   14.30  (-------*------)
AN      20  158.92   31.03                  (------*-------)
BF      20  172.83   44.29                       (------*-------)
YM      20  154.46   33.33              (------*------)
                            ---+---------+---------+---------+------
                             120       140       160       180

Pooled StDev = 32.56
```

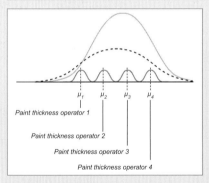

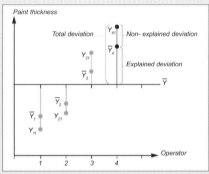

Analyzing the results
- **Step 1**: Check the significance of the main effect ("Operator") using the p-value (here: significance is given)

- **Step 2**: Check the amount of explained deviation ($SS_{Factor\ levels}$) using the R-Sq.
$R\text{-}Sq = SS_{Factor\ level} / SS_{Total} \cdot 100\%$
(here: the amount of the explained deviation is too small, less than 20%)

- **Step 3**: Check the validity of the model analysing the residuals (for more details on the residual analysis see the chapter about linear regression). Since the residuals in the example are not normally distributed the significance tests (and respective p-value) are invalid and cannot be trusted. Non-normal residuals are an indicator of incomplete models, i. e. further important factors have not been included in the model.

Example of Residual Plots for Paint Thickness

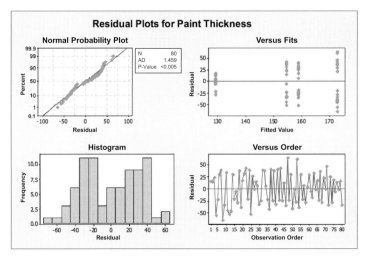

Two-Factorial ANOVA

☐ Terms
Two-factorial ANOVA, two-way ANOVA

◷ When
In the Analyze Phase

◎ Goal
Examine the effect and interaction of two independent, discrete factors on continuous, dependent output variables.

▶▶ Steps
Analogous to the one-factorial model, the total deviation is the addition of the squared sums of the individual factors, the squared sum of the factor interactions, and the squared sum of the errors (spread within the factors).

Total deviation = explained deviation + non-explained deviation

$$SS_T = SS_A + SS_B + SS_{AB} + SS_\varepsilon$$

Total sum of the squares

Sum of the squares from factor A

Sum of the squares from factor B

Sum of the squares from the error

Sum of the squares from the interactions between factors A and B

If the sum of the squares from the factors and the factor interactions is significantly greater than the spread within the factor, then a difference exists and the null hypotheses can be rejected. Model:

$$y_{ijk} = \mu + \tau_i + \beta_j + (\tau\beta)_{ij} + \varepsilon_{ijk}$$

k-th observation under the i-th factor level of factor A and the j-th factor level of factor B

Total mean value

Effect of the i-th factor level of factor A

Effect of the j-th factor level of factor B

Random error

Effect generated by the interaction

The hypotheses are formed analogous to the one-factor model:

The hypothesis for the effect of factor A is:
$H_0: \tau_1 = \tau_2 = \ldots = \tau_I = 0$
H_A: at least one $\tau_i \neq 0$

The hypothesis for the effect of factor B is:
$H_0: \beta_1 = \beta_2 = \ldots = \beta_J = 0$
H_A: at least one $\beta_j \neq 0$

The hypothesis for the effect of the interactions is:
$H_0: (\tau\beta)_{ij} = 0$ for all i, j
H_A: at least one $(\tau\beta)_{ij} \neq 0$

Example of Two-Factorial Variance Analysis

Two-way ANOVA: Paint thickness versus Paint box; Operator

```
Analysis of variance for paint thickness
Source          DF          SS         MS         F          P
Paint box        1       62304    62303.9     512.58      0.000
Operator         3       19853     6617.8      54.44      0.000
Interaction      3        9515     3171.7      26.09      0.000
Error           72        8752      121.6
Total           79      100424
```

Analyzing the results
- **Step 1**: *Visualize the amplitude of the main effects and interactions and check their significance using the p-value (here: significance is given for all main effects and the interaction)*

Continuation "Analyzing the results" on Page 175.

DEFINE

MEASURE

ANALYZE

IMPROVE

CONTROL

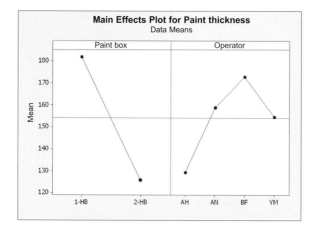

Result:
the main effects of both factors are visible here.

In box 1 the paint is considerably thicker on average than in box 2.

Operator AH produces on average the least thickness, whereas BF is responsible for the thickest application.

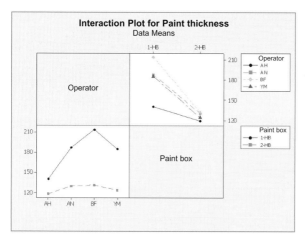

Result:
the factor interactions are depicted here.

Operator BF produces a thickness of 210 µm on average when working from box 1. This is almost double that of operator AH. The difference is smaller when both work from box 2.

BF should thus no longer work from box 1.

Analyzing the results (continued)
- **Step 2a**: Check the significance of the main effects ("operator" and "paint box") using the p-value (here: significance is given for both)

- **Step 2b**: Check the amount of explained deviation ($SS_{Factor\ levels} + SS_{Interactions}$) using the R-Sq.
  $R\text{-}Sq = (SS_{Paint\ Box} + SS_{Operator} + SS_{Interaction})/SS_{Total} \cdot 100\%$
  (here: the amount of explained deviation is very high, above 90%)

- **Step 3**: Check the validity of the model analysing the residuals (for more details on the residual analysis see the chapter on linear regression). The null hypothesis of normally distributed residuals must be rejected. We expect to have further relevant factors that significantly influence the paint thickness.

Example of Residual Plots for Paint Thickness

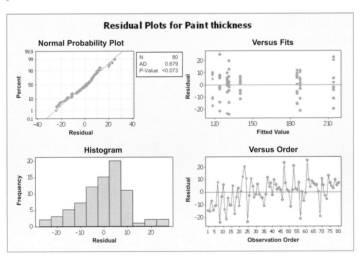

Correlation Coefficient

📁 **Term**
Correlation coefficient

🕐 **When**
In the Analyze Phase

◎ **Goal**
Measure the strength of linear relationship between two continuous variables.

▶▶ **Steps**
The correlation coefficient as formulated by Bravais-Pearson is a measure for determining the strength of the linear relationship between two continuous variables:

$$r_{xy} = \frac{s_{xy}}{s_x \cdot s_y} = \frac{\sum\limits_{i=1}^{n}(x_i - \bar{x})(y_i - \bar{y})}{\sqrt{\sum\limits_{i=1}^{n}(x_i - \bar{x})^2 \cdot \sum\limits_{i=1}^{n}(y_i - \bar{y})^2}}$$

The correlation coefficient can assume values between -1 and +1:

$$-1 \le r_{xy} \le +1$$

The correlations can be classified roughly as follows (rule of thumb):

$|r_{xy}| \cong 0 \Rightarrow$ *no correlation, no linear relationship*

$|r_{xy}| < 0.5 \Rightarrow$ *"weak correlation"*

$0.5 \le |r_{xy}| < 0.8 \Rightarrow$ *"moderate correlation"*

$0.8 \le |r_{xy}| \Rightarrow$ *"strong correlation"*

$|r_{xy}| \cong 1 \Rightarrow$ *perfect correlation*

⇨ **Tips**

- The correlation coefficient is able to recognize linear correlation. Non-linear relationships remain unconsidered here. The calculated correlation coefficient assumes a value around "0" in these cases. This merely says that there is no linear relationship. Analyzing the data on graphs in advance is therefore always recommended.

- The correlation coefficient can only capture a relationship between two variables, not the direction of an effect in the sense of the influence exerted by an input factor on the output (if A is dependent on B, or B on A). The effect of one variable on another variable can only be determined by very specific deliberations and not from the dimension of the correlation coefficient.

- If a high correlation exists between two characteristics which is not justified in terms of content, then we have a pseudo-correlation. Pseudo-relationships of this type can be generated by a third characteristic highly correlated with the two observed ones being overlooked and remaining unconsidered.

Example of a Correlation Coefficient
Example: correlation

```
Correlations: Paint thickness; amount of thinner (in %)

Pearson correlation of paint thickness and amount of
thinner(in %) = -0.987
P-Value = 0.000
```

Result:
There appears to be a strong negative relationship between the proportions of the thinner and the paint thickness.

The p-value indicates that the null hypothesis (independence between the variables) has to be rejected.

Simple Linear Regression

☐ Term
Simple linear regression

⊙ When
In the Analyze Phase

◎ Goals
– Analyze the relationship between a continuous, independent variable and a continuous, dependent output.
– Determine a linear function with the capability of explaining as many data points as possible, and to minimize the data deviation (residuals) from the function.

⏵⏵ Steps
The Regression Analysis describes the relationship between a dependent and an independent variable as a function:

$$y = f(x)$$

The simple linear regression model has the form:

$$Y = b_0 + b_1 x + \varepsilon$$

Dependent variable   Error term (residuals)

Regression   Axis intercept   Independent variable (regressor)
coefficients   Gradient of the regression line

The error term corresponds to the deviation that is not explained by the variable. These deviations are accidental and may be interpreted as variations in materials or measurement errors. The expected value of the error term is zero.
The regression coefficients are predicted through the least square method. The parameters are determined in such a way that the predicted line minimizes the sum of the squared residuals.

The predicted line has the following form:

$$\hat{y} = \hat{b}_0 + \hat{b}_1 x$$

The deviation between the observed value of y_i and the predicted $\hat{y}_i$ is the residual ε_i.

$$\varepsilon_i = y_i - \hat{y}_i$$

▶▶ **Steps**
− Formulate the model.
  Concrete aspects take priority:
  - Does the cause-and-effect relationship make sense?
  - Have all of the variables been considered and is the model complete?
− Predict the regression function with the aid of statistics software.
− Test the predicted regression function:
  - Do the predicted values make sense (check the signs)?
  - Is the predicted model statistically significant?
  - Are the predicted coefficients statistically significant?
  - Does the predicted model fulfill the necessary model assumptions and/or prerequisites?

Test the predicted regression function
− *Coefficient of determination (R²):*
  Indicates the proportion of the explained deviation on the total deviation, i.e. the percentage of variation from y that can be explained through the model.

$$R^2 = 1 - \frac{SS_{Regression}}{SS_{Total}} = 1 - \frac{\sum_{i=1}^{n}(\hat{y}_i - \bar{y})^2}{\sum_{i=1}^{n}(y_i - \bar{y})^2}$$

− *F-test:*
  This test answers the question whether the predicted model is also valid for the population and not just the sample. The model is statistically significant when this is the case.

The corresponding null hypothesis is: "There is no relationship and thus the regression coefficients in the population are all equally zero".

$$F = \frac{MS_{Regression}}{MS_{Error}}$$

– *Regression coefficients:*
The regression coefficients are tested for their significance through t-tests. The hypotheses are:

H_0: $b_0 = 0$ The line intersects the origin.
H_A: $b_0 \neq 0$ The line does not intersect the origin.
H_0: $b_i = 0$ There is no relationship between the independent variable x_i and the dependent variable y.
H_A: $b_i \neq 0$ There is a relationship between the independent variable x_i and the dependent variable y.

– *Analysis of residuals:*
The analysis of residuals on the graphs provides us with important indicators on how well the model fits. The existence of trends and the dependency of one variable on another indicate that the model is incomplete or false. Furthermore, the model is based on the assumption that the residuals are normally distributed. Violation of this assumption is decisive: The test statistic and procedure are no longer applicable.

Example of Trend/Autocorrelation of Residuals
Example: residuals over time/observation numbers

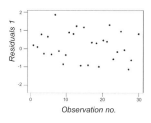

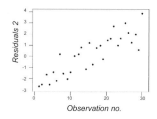

No trend evident!
Residuals do not change over time (no autocorrelation).

Trend evident!
Residuals become larger over time (autocorrelation). This indicates that factors yet to be captured are changing the results, e.g. machinery wearout, outside temperatures, etc.

Example of Residual Variance

Example: residuals vs. predicted model value (ŷ)

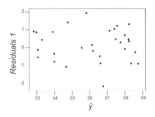

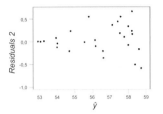

Standard deviation and variance are constant (homoskedasticity).

The standard deviation increases with the calculated y-value, the residuals lie within a funnel form. Standard deviation and variance are not constant (heteroskedasticity).

Example of Normal Distribution

Example: "normal plot of residuals" and "histogram of residuals"

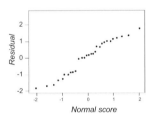

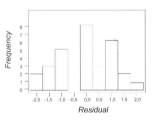

If the residuals are normally distributed they lie roughly on a line in a normal plot and the histogram has the shape of a bell curve.

If this is not clearly apparent from the graphs, a normality test needs to be carried out for the residuals.

DEFINE

MEASURE

ANALYZE

IMPROVE

CONTROL

Example of Simple Linear Regression

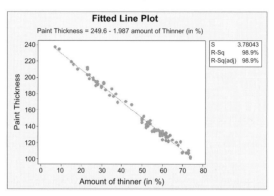

Fitted Line Plot

Paint Thickness = 249.6 - 1.987 amount of Thinner (in %)

S	3.78043
R-Sq	98.9%
R-Sq(adj)	98.9%

The Fitted Line Plot generates the regression function that best fits and explains the underlying data and represents these in a graph.

Multiple Linear Regression

🗀 **Term**

Multiple linear regression

🕐 **When**

In the Analyze Phase

◎ **Goals**
- Analyze the effect of more than one independent variable on a dependent variable.
- Determine a function that best explains this effect.

▶▶ **Steps**

The regression function has the following general form:

$$Y = b_0 + b_1 X_1 + b_2 X_2 + \ldots + b_n X_n + \varepsilon$$

An important prerequisite for the multiple linear regression is the independence of the explanative variables x_i (no multicollinearity).

Example: Example of independence check of the x_i

Example: independence of the explanative variables x_i (regressors)

This graph enables a visual examination of the relationship between the input variables and the output (paint thickness vs. thinner amount and paint thickness vs. temperature) as well as between the two input variables (thinner amount vs. temperature).

It is expected that there is a relationship between the input and output (here: paint thickness and thinner).

But between the input variables independence is the prerequisite for regression (here: thinner vs. temperature).

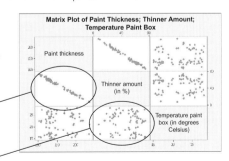

Matrix Plot of Paint Thickness; Thinner Amount; Temperature Paint Box

Paint thickness

Thinner amount (in %)

Temperature paint box (in degrees Celsius)

DEFINE

MEASURE

ANALYZE

IMPROVE

CONTROL

Example Multiple Linear Regression

Result:

Through the high coefficient of determination R^2 and the significant F-test we can assume that this model will furnish a suitably good explanation of the relationship. As expected, the amount of thinner has an influence on paint thickness, the temperature though it is not significant (see p-value).

```
Regression analysis: paint thickness versus thinner amount (; temperature
paint box

The regression equation is
Paint thickness = 251 - 1.99 thinner amount (in %)
              - 0.067 Temperature paint box (in degrees Cel)

Predictor                      Coef     SE Coef        T       P      VIF
Constant                    251.173       2.675    93.91   0.000
Thinner amount (in %)       -1.98909     0.02410   -82.54   0.000    1.0
Temperature paint box
(in degrees Cel)             -0.0671      0.1043    -0.64   0.522    1.0

S = 3.79472    R-Sq = 98.9%    R-Sq(adj) = 98.9%

Analysis of variance

Source          DF        SS        MS        F        P
Regression       2     99315     49658   3448.47    0.000
Residual Error  77      1109        14
Total           79    100424
```

Tip: The VIF (Variance Inflation Factor) hints at the independence of the regressors. A VIF close to 1 means that there is no multicollinearity (i.e. the regressors are independent); a VIF of approx. 5 or more indicates strong multicollinearity.

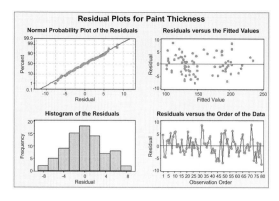

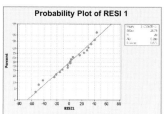

Analysis of residuals:
The graph analysis of residuals reveals no patterns. A normality test can be carried out to be sure (here: the null hypothesis cannot be rejected).

Design of Experiments (DOE)

📁 **Term**
Design of experiments (DOE)

🕐 **When**
In Analyze, during the transition to Improve

◎ **Goals**
- Undertake a systematic procedure in the sense of an efficient process analysis.
- Work out the relationship between the influencing factors in a process and the resulting product and process qualities with a minimal number of experiments.
- Determine the optimal settings for establishing the response within the customer specifications.

▶▶ **Steps**
1. Define the optimization task and set the responses.
2. Identify the influencing variables.
3. Determine the relevant factor levels.
4. Derive the experiment strategy: Set the suitable design and sample size.
5. Ensure the measurement capability.
6. Conduct experiments and collect data.
7. Analyze the results and derive actions.

1. **Define the optimization task and set the responses**
   - Select the product or process for analysis.
   - Set the goals.
   - Set the responses for measuring whether the goals are achieved.
   - Make sure that the responses have the following characteristics:
     - Completeness: All the key process and product characteristics are covered.
     - Dissimilarity: Each response describes a different relationship.
     - Relevance: Each response has a clear relationship to the goal of the analysis.

- Linearity: If there are several similar responses, select the one that depends linearly on the influencing variables.
- Quantification: Wherever possible the responses should be continuous or metric.

2. **Identify the influencing variables**
   - Identify the decisive influencing variables with the aid of structured brainstorming. The most important aids are:
     - Cause & effect diagram
     - Tool 3
     - FMEA
   - Results gained in the process and data analysis can be taken into account:
     - Analysis of variance
     - Regression analysis
   - The final evaluation should be based on the following criteria:
     - Importance of a factor
     - Accuracy of a possible setting
     - Reproducibility of the setting
     - Effort and expense in changing the levels

3. **Determine the relevant factor levels**
   - A maximum and minimum are set as factor levels. Two factor levels are selected initially:
     - Continuous variables: The maximum and minimum should lie in a sensible area so that the response is still quantifiable.
     - Discrete variables: If the factor levels are discrete, e.g. there are five producers, refer initially to the two most important factor levels.

4. **Derive the experiment strategy**
   - Set the sample sizes (plan the experiment scope).
   - Determine the number of blocks.
   - Decide on randomization or take into consideration restrictions in randomization (e.g. due to the costs of the experimental setup).
   - Determine the factor level combinations: Full-factorial or fractional factorial DOE.
   - Normally a full-factorial DOE is very expensive and time-consuming. To ensure the best relationship between costs and information quality a successive procedure is recommended as follows:

DOE

DEFINE

MEASURE

ANALYZE

IMPROVE

CONTROL

- *Block 0: Good-bad trials*
  - There are two different settings for each factor, which lead to distinctly different values of the observed target values. The settings can be characterized as "good" or "bad" by experts (adjusted factors).
  - All of the factors are set in such a way that a "good" result can be expected, e.g. low error rate, high concentration of agents. All of the factors are then set so that a "bad" result can be expected, e.g. high error rate, low concentration of agents.
  - The goal is to ascertain whether there are any effects at all. If no effects are located this can be due to the fact that the selected factors are not relevant or the signal-noise relationship is too weak, i.e. the noise is too "loud". At this point the experiments should be discontinued and, if required, further factors should be determined or the noise should be eliminated.

- *Block 1: Screening experiments*
  - It is common that 10 or even up to 15 factors are selected.
  - If effects exist in principle experiments with resolution III or IV should be carried out at first.
  - The important question here is, "Are there effects of a sufficient dimension?"
  - The goal is to locate the relevant factors in this phase ("Separate the wheat from the chaff"). It is often possible to significantly reduce the number of relevant factors and conduct further DOEs based on far fewer experiments.
  - When deciding to leave out factors attention needs to be paid to possible interactions. In practice we therefore avoid reducing factors in a resolution III.

- *Block 2: Fold-over experiments*
  Fold-over experiments supplement screening DOEs through a complementary plan. This is a reversal of the signs deployed in the starting DOE.
  - The goal is to reduce the number of factors to the really important ones. This makes it possible to estimate the interactions. Fold-over experiments eliminate any confounding between the main effects and interactions.

- • The statistical analysis can provide the beginnings for the optimal settings (Response Optimizer).

- *Block 3: Completion experiments*
  - • If there is reason to assume that the relationships are non-linear, i.e. squared effects exist or effects of a higher order, additional experiments are carried out which, besides the minimum and maximum settings, take into consideration additional mean values.
  - • This is known as the response surface methodology (e.g. central composite design).

- *Block 4: Optimization experiments*
  - • Optimal settings are proposed when analyzing the statistics generated by the preceding experiments.
  - • The goal now is to test the optimal settings of the factors.

Estimate the costs: make sure that the costs are reasonable in relation to the hoped-for results.
If the expense appears to be too great, then examine whether the costs can be reduced by doing without factors and factor levels, by block building or randomization, or carrying out a smaller number of experiments – without, of course, endangering the goal. If this proves unfeasible it may prove necessary to rethink the goal.

5. **Ensure the measurement capability**
   - – Develop the operational definition and carry out a measurement system analysis.
   - – A measurement system analysis verifies if the measurement system is suitable. Improve the system whenever required.

6. **Conduct experiments and collect data**
   - – Prior to actually conducting the experiments it is recommended to carry out a couple of preliminary tests or pilots.
     The goal is to see whether the estimated expense and effort is realistic, and the result is consistent, i.e. the noise has been eliminated.
   - – When conducting the experiments make sure that everything runs according to plan. This means that each of the experiments has to be monitored individually.

7. **Analyze the results and derive the measures**
   - The statistical analysis of the results proceeds according to the methodologies of the regression (least square) and variance analysis.
   - The graph and analytical results are reviewed after each block so as to determine the next steps. In this respect, carrying out DOE is an *iterative process*.
   - When analyzing the results and deciding on the next steps, one or several experts involved in the process should always be consulted so as to avoid drawing misleading conclusions. Such conclusions can conceal the true relationships, e.g. through measurement errors or noise. The results need to be checked at all times to see if they make sense.

Full-Factorial Design

☐ Term
Full-factorial design

⊙ When
In Analyze, during the transition to Improve

◎ Goal
Determine the effect of the main factors and factor interactions by systematically testing all factor combinations.

▶▶ Steps
In the following, some terms and concepts will be presented.

Factors and factor levels
Factors are influencing variables. In factorial DOE the factor levels are reduced to their extreme values (realistic minimal and maximal values). This step ensures that the largest possible area is covered at justifiable costs and efforts.

The mean value of a factor level initially holds less information than the extreme values. The mean value is only of greater significance for non-linear relationships.
A DOE has the form of 2^k, i.e. k factors each with 2 factor levels (minimum and maximum).

Repeats and replicates
– With *repeat,* we denote the immediate repeating of an experiment without changing the settings. No other settings are carried out between the repeats.
  - Repeats capture short-term variation.
  - Repeats require no new experiment setup.
  - Repeats do not generate any additional degrees of freedom in the design.
– Replicates mean that the entire experiment setup with all its settings is reproduced completely.

190

- Replicates increase the number of degrees of freedom in the design.
- Replicates increase the sample size.
- Replicates enable us to capture long-term variation.
- Replicates increase the required number of experimental setups.

Size of the required sample
The following rule of thumb has proven suitable for experimental designs:

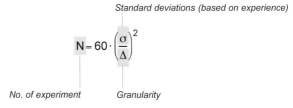

Standard deviations (based on experience)

$$N = 60 \cdot \left(\frac{\sigma}{\Delta}\right)^2$$

No. of experiment   *Granularity*

In addition, m is the number of single experiments in a design and N the number of replicates. Accordingly, n can be calculated as follows:

$$n = \frac{N}{m}$$

In practice the number of experiments is limited by the time and budget considerations.

Control parameters and noise factors
- Control parameters are the dimensions that can be set and maintained at a desired value. Control parameters should be set in such a way that the noise has as little impact as possible, meaning that we have a robust process.
- Noise factors can be either known or unknown. Known noise factors need to be eliminated or included in the experimental design as a factor. If this proves impossible, the effect they generate can be eliminated through block building. Adjustments cannot be made for unknown noise factors. They represent the background noise. Randomization can minimize their effect.

Randomization and block building
- Randomization means that the individual experiments in each block are conducted in a random sequence. Randomization neutralizes trends which arise through disturbances (noise) and can falsify the result. The random sequence is created with the aid of random numbers.

DEFINE

MEASURE

ANALYZE

IMPROVE

CONTROL

DEFINE

MEASURE

ANALYZE

IMPROVE

CONTROL

  – Block building is the assignment of individual experiments into blocks. Block building takes into consideration known noise factors, e.g. different temperatures and / or humidity at various times of day during production.

Balanced (saturated) design
The same number of positive and negative signs (minimal and maximum-settings) is taken into consideration for each factor.

Full-factorial design
Full-factorial design means that all the factor levels of all the factors are combined with one another. This allows us to cover all interactions. For a DOE with three factors the basic pattern of a design would be as follows:

No.	*Factors*			*Factor interactions*			
	A	B	C	AB	AC	BC	ABC
1	-	-	-	+	+	+	-
2	+	-	-	-	-	+	+
3	-	+	-	-	+	-	+
4	+	+	-	+	-	-	-
5	-	-	+	+	-	-	+
6	+	-	+	-	+	-	-
7	-	+	+	-	-	+	-
8	+	+	+	+	+	+	+

The advantage gained by full-factorial design is that it enables all information to be captured and analyzed. However, due to the cost and time involved it is not always feasible: the number of experiments increases exponentially as the number of factors increases.

Calculating effects
The following equation is used to calculate the main effects and the effects generated by interactions:

$$\text{Effect} = \begin{array}{c}\text{Mean value of the response}\\\text{when factor setting at}\\\text{the high level}\\(Y_A+)\end{array} - \begin{array}{c}\text{Mean value of the response}\\\text{when factor setting at}\\\text{the low level}\\(Y_A-)\end{array}$$

Analyzing DOE

1. Analyze the collected data with the aid of suitable statistic programs such as Minitab®.
2. Determine the factors and the interactions.
3. Remove statistically insignificant effects from the model (as a rule effects with a p-value bigger than 0.1) and repeat the analysis.
4. Analyze residuals to make sure that the model is correctly set *(cf. analysis of residuals)*.
5. Examine and analyze the significant interactions and main effects on graphs (interaction plot, main effects plot) and set up the mathematical model.
6. Translate the model into practical conclusions and derive the suitable measures.

Example of Full-Factorial DOE

Example: car dealer

No.	Temperature	Pressure	Thinner	Result
1	20	15	10	152
2	25	15	10	167
3	20	30	10	180
4	25	30	10	159
5	20	15	20	198
6	25	15	20	201
7	20	30	20	230
8	25	30	20	236

DEFINE

MEASURE

ANALYZE

IMPROVE

CONTROL

Fractional Factorial Design

▢ Term
Fractional factorial design

◷ When
In Analyze, during the transition to Improve

◎ Goals
− Locate the relationship between the influencing factors in a process and the resulting product and process characteristics.
− Minimize the number of experiments.

▶▶ Steps
Fractional factorial design considerably reduces the number of experiments while ensuring that the information lost is minimal.

Loss of information is accepted initially. By extending the design (Fold Over) the information lost can be retrieved later.

Besides wanting to save time and keeping costs low, not all of the factor interactions are of interest. Further experimental setups can always be deployed afterwards should the initial results demand more precise information.

A fractional factorial DOE has the form of 2^{k-q}, with q being the reduction factor.

To ensure that the design remains saturated (balanced) the same number of positive and negative signs needs to be considered. The signs are selected so that a sensible interpretation is possible. With four factors the following basic pattern emerges:

Signs of ABC

No.	A	B	C	D	AB	AC	BC	ABC
1	-	-	-	-	+	+	+	-
2	+	-	-	+	-	-	+	+
3	-	+	-	+	-	+	-	+
4	+	+	-	-	+	-	-	-
5	-	-	+	+	+	-	-	+
6	+	-	+	-	-	+	-	-
7	-	+	+	-	-	-	+	-
8	+	+	+	+	+	+	+	+
9	-	-	-	+	...	...	...	...
...	...	...	...	...	...	...	...	...

The signs of factor D are therefore replaced by the signs of the interaction ABC. We can take this step because of the extremely small probability that these three factors influence one another simultaneously. This ensures that we can deduce the effect of factor D. Of course it is still remotely possible that the interaction ABC is significant and that factor D is only interpreted as significant for this reason.

Confounding and resolution types

Confounding means that the columns in a fractional factorial design are the same; if this is the case we cannot distinguish between the effects.

Resolution types:

		No. of factors												
		2	3	4	5	6	7	8	9	10	11	12	13	14	15
No. of experiments	4	Full	III												
	8		Full	IV	III	III	III								
	16			Full	V	IV	IV	IV	III	III	III	III	III	III	III
	32				Full	VI	IV	IV	IV	IV	IV	IV	IV	IV	IV
	64					Full	VII	V	IV	IV	IV	IV	IV	IV	IV
	128						Full	VIII	VI	V	V	IV	IV	IV	IV

Resolution type	Confounding	Evaluation
III	Main factors are confounded with two-factor interaction	Critical
IV	Main factors with three-factor interaction / two-factor interaction with two-factor interaction	Less critical
V	Main factors with four-factor interaction / two-factor interaction with three-factor interaction	Non-critical

The analysis occurs in the same steps as in a full-factorial design.

Example of Fractional Factorial DOE

Example: car dealer

No.	Temperature	Pressure	Thinner	Paint box	Result
1	20	15	10	1	152
2	25	15	10	2	167
3	20	30	10	2	180
4	25	30	10	1	159
5	20	15	20	2	198
6	25	15	20	1	201
7	20	30	20	1	230
8	25	30	20	2	236
9	-	-	-	-	-
...	-	-	-	-	-

Variation Reduction

🗀 **Term**

Variation reduction

🕒 **When**

In Analyze, during the transition to Improve

◎ **Goal**

Determine at which standard deviation or variance setting the smallest variation occurs as a response.

▶▶ **Steps**

- Calculate the standard deviation or variance. This enables the calculation of the variation of each setting. Two new responses are defined: one for location (e.g. mean) and one for the variation (e.g. standard deviation).
- Observing the standard deviation as a response allows the relevant factors influencing the variation to be identified with simple tools and the classical factorial DOE; the variation reduction can proceed on this basis.
- To stabilize the variation it is necessary to transform the variance. Usually either the root transformation (in this case the result is standard deviation) or the logarithmic transformation (ln – natural logarithm) is applied.
- For considering standard deviation as response, several measurements are necessary by repeats.

The setup and analysis follows that used in factorial designs.

Example of Variation Reduction

Factors and factor settings				Results of repeats					Mean and standard deviation	
A	B	C	D	M 1	M 2	M 3	M 4	M 5	Mean	Standard deviation
+	-	+	+							
-	-	+	+							

Response Surface Methodology

☐ Term
Response surface methodology (RSM)

⊘ When
In Analyze, during the transition to Improve as an optimization experiment

◎ Goals
– Integrate non-linear relationships.
– Additionally optimize the response with a specific setting of factors.

▶▶ Steps
– Reduce the number of factors as far as possible by full factorial fractional functional designs and continue to observe only the genuinely relevant factors. This demands more experiments because not only extreme values are examined but also mean values.

– Taking into consideration the non-linear relationships, the following model describes the curvature of the surface:

$$y = b_0 + b_1 x_1 + b_2 x_2 + b_{11} (x_1)^2 + b_{22} (x_2)^2 + b_{12} x_1 x_2$$

Response
y-axis section ———— Coefficient of the factors ————

To determine the additional coefficients we require the mean values between the extreme points of the factors. Here we apply for example the central composite design (CCD).

The analysis generally follows the same steps as that of the other designs. However, it can be expected that at least one non-linear relationship is significant.

DEFINE

MEASURE

ANALYZE

IMPROVE

CONTROL

Analyze Closure Matrix

📁 **Term**

Analyze closure matrix

🕐 **When**

At the end of the Analyze Phase

◎ **Goals**
- Define the root causes.
- Assess whether the root causes form a sufficient lever.

▶▶ **Steps**
- List all suspected causes.
- Depict the verification strategy with result.
- List the root causes and the potential generated by future improvement or elimination.

Example of an Analyze Closure Matrix

Suspected Root Cause	Verified through...	Root Causes	Potential
• Impure nozzles lead to a poor paint application	• Experimental design with impure and new nozzles. Verify the paint results. The error pattern occurs with the impure nozzles.	• Impure nozzles	• Solution to the defective application of paint thickness. Approx. € 30,000 p.a.
...	...	...	...
...	...	...	...

Checklist for the Analyze Phase

Potential Causes
The possible causes for the problem are identified. ☑

The possible causes are categorized and prioritized. ☑

Verification of Potential Causes: Process Analysis
The current process is analyzed and the weak points are identified. ☑

Value and time analyses have been carried out. ☑

Verification of Potential Causes: Data Analysis
The key input and process measurements are identified. ☑

The data quality (e.g. through a Gage R & R) is ensured. ☑

The data gathered is analyzed with the aid of suitable statistical methods. ☑

Root Causes
A list of verified causes is drawn up. ☑

Project Charter
The project goal and scope are reviewed and adjusted if necessary. ☑

The expected net benefit is reviewed and adjusted if necessary. ☑

Analyze
Carry out the Gate Review. ☑

DEFINE

MEASURE

ANALYZE

IMPROVE

CONTROL

Six Sigma^{+Lean} Toolset

IMPROVE

Phase 4: Improve

Goals

– Generate solutions based on the root causes.
– Select the best solutions – taking into consideration benefit and effort – which contribute to achieving the goal.
– Secure the implementation of the measures derived from the solutions.

Steps

– Gather and elaborate possible solutions using the creativity techniques as well as the proven methods and tools of lean management and best practice.
– Evaluate and select solutions capable of improving the process.
– Develop and plan measures for implementing the solutions.
– Optional: Carry out a pilot program.

Tools

- **Theory of Constraints (TOC)**
- **5 S**
- **Setup Time Reduction**
- **Generic Pull System**
- **Replenishment Pull System**
- **Poka Yoke**
- **Total Productive Maintenance (TPM)**
- **Lean for Service**
- **Creativity Techniques**
- **Tools for Selecting Solutions**
- **Implementation Planning**
- **Pilot Program**
- **Roll Out Planning**

List of Root Causes

1	
2	
3	
...	

Generate Solutions

Brainstorming + Lean

Select Solutions

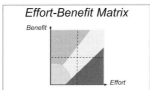

Effort-Benefit Matrix

Draw up Should-be Process

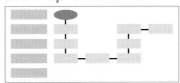

Carry out Pilot

ACT | PLAN
CHECK | DO

Carry out Roll Out

	Jan.	Feb.	March	April
	1	2	3	4
1				
1.1				
1.2				
2				
2.1				
2.2				
3				
3.1				
3.2				
4				

DEFINE

MEASURE

ANALYZE

IMPROVE

CONTROL

Theory of Constraints (TOC)

☐ Term
Theory of constraints (based on Eliyahu M. Goldratt and Robert Fox)

◔ When
In the Improve Phase, generating solutions

◎ Goal
Systematic concentration on constraints in the company.

▶▶ Steps
– The basis is given by the system definition of cybernetics:
A system comprises elements which interact with one another and are separated from other elements and systems. Economic systems are only successful when they grow. For this reason, when analyzing a system TOC concentrates on the boundaries of the observed system.

– TOC observes the process as a chain made up of many links.

– The performance of the whole chain is determined by the performance of its weakest link.

– Three key indicators are focused on and optimized:
- **Exit rate:** ⟶
  The more the better.
  $$\frac{\text{Sales price - variable costs}}{\text{Time}}$$

- **Inventories:**
  The less the better.

- **Operating costs:**
  All expenses to produce (without considering allocation to single areas).
  The less the better.
  (Operating expenses are viewed as fixed costs.)

- Apply the TOC concept to focus on constraints:
  1. Identify the constraint.
  2. Exploit the constraint.
  3. Subordinate everything else to the constraint.
  4. Elevate the constraint.
  5. Identify the next constraint: Go back to Step 1.

⇨ **Tip**

Eliyahu M. Goldratt and Robert Fox began developing the Theory of Constraints in 1980 as the basis for their consultancy activities, first publishing their findings and experiences as *"What is this thing called theory of constraints"* in 1990. The approach primarily gained renown with Goldratt's novel of business life *"The goal"*.

DEFINE

MEASURE

ANALYZE

IMPROVE

CONTROL

DEFINE

MEASURE

ANALYZE

IMPROVE

CONTROL

5 S

☐ Term

5 S: Sort – Seiri; Set in order – Seiton; Shine – Seiso; Standardize – Seiketsu; Sustain – Shitsuke.

◷ When

In the Improve Phase, generating solutions

◎ Goals

– Create and maintain an organized, clean and efficient working environment that is the basis for optimized processes.
– Prompt evaluation of your working environment as to whether normal conditions predominate.
– Direct integration and participation of all employees so as to generate a sense of responsibility that is sustainable in the long term.

▶▶ Steps

Sort – Seiri

– *In general:* Sort through and mark all materials and objects in the working environment; sort out those materials which are not directly required.
– Attach red dots or tags to materials, which are not directly required ("red tagging"). Keep the materials in a marked zone for a defined period of time.
– After this period, the marked objects and materials are to be:
  - removed completely if they are tagged as "unnecessary", i.e. they are to be sold or disposed.
  - kept if they are tagged as "required".
  If you are not sure, follow the rule: "When in doubt throw it out!"

Example of "Red Tagging"

RED TAG	
Number	
Date	
Division	
Type	☐ Machine
	☐ Tool
	☐ Document
	☐ Other (please describe below)
Description	
Amount	
Value	
What was done: scrapped ☐, sold ☐, moved to another place ☐, left at the same place ☐	
Date of action	

Set in order – Seiton
– Arrange and label objects so that anyone can find them and return them to the correct place.
– Sort the objects and give them a "permanent place' that is labeled accordingly.
– Use aids:
  - Colored markings for defined areas
  - "Home addresses" to be able to assign objects to definite areas
  - Labels designating the object and its storage place
– Utilize the principles of economy of movement.

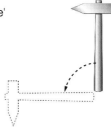

Shine – Seiso
– Remove dirt and other impurities as well as scraps and waste materials in the immediate working environment.
– Define the cleaning goals and the areas to be cleaned.
– Draw up, and distribute a schedule and define responsibilities.
– Define procedures for regular cleaning activities.
– Schedule audits and set their goals.

DEFINE

MEASURE

ANALYZE

IMPROVE

CONTROL

Standardize – Seiketsu
– Create a consistent procedure for things that have to be carried out on a daily basis, like sort, set in order, and shine.
– "Do things the right way at all times!"

Sustain – Shitsuke
– Integrate the 5 S mentality generated into everyday work and all processes.
– 5 S should not degenerate into a one-time action ("flavor of the day").
– Integrate 5 S audit forms for collecting and presenting results (radar chart).
– Establish a regular audit cycle to ensure sustainability.

⇨ **Tip**
Take photos of the area before and after the 5 S actions. *(An example is given on p. 273)*

Example of Sustain

	Sort	Set in order	Shine	Standardize	Sustain
Current	75%	65%	75%	95%	65%
Goal	100%	100%	95%	100%	95%
Next audit					

An organized, clean and efficient working environment
– is more productive,
– causes fewer problems and loss of information,
– enhances the ability to meet schedules,
– is a more reliable and safer workplace.

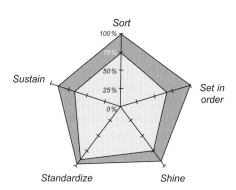

Setup Time Reduction

📁 **Term**

Setup time reduction, SMED (Single Minute Exchange of Die), 4-Step Methodology

🕓 **When**

In the Improve Phase, generating solutions

◎ **Goals**
- Reduce lead time at constraints with the opportunity to reduce batch sizes.
- Arrange production flexibly to be able to meet different customer demands.
- Achieve an accelerated introduction of design changes.

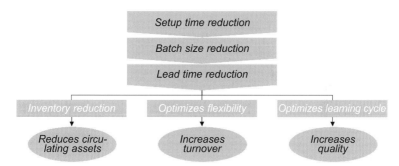

▶▶ **Steps**

Definition of setup time

The duration between the last good part of a batch and the first good part of the following batch with the planned process speed.

Level 1:

Document the setup process and divide activities into internal and external activities
- Internal setup activities: activities, which can only be accomplished when the machine is shut down (e.g. changing moulds and tools).
- External setup activities: activities, which can be accomplished while the machine is still operating (preparing materials, boot a tool program).

DEFINE

MEASURE

ANALYZE

IMPROVE

CONTROL

DEFINE

MEASURE

ANALYZE

IMPROVE

CONTROL

Example: Definition of Setup Time

Preparation Setup Adjustment   Trial runs

Last good part
of a batch

First good part of
following batch

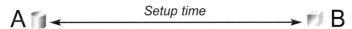

A ←————— *Setup time* —————→ B

*Setup time is defined as the interval between the last good part
of a batch and the first good part of following batch.*

Level 2:

Convert internal into external activities

– A great deal of time is lost during setup activities through searching for
  materials and information.
– Focus on activities, which delay or disrupt the process flow. Carry out a
  detailed analysis of the reasons for disruption.
– Carry out a brainstorming to identify opportunities for converting internal
  into external activities.

No.	Spray-painting setup process [Description]	Time needed [Minutes]	Activity Internal	External
1	Fix spoiler	2	2	
2	Mix paint	1	1	
3	Clean spray gun	7	7	
4	Attach / setup nozzle	5		5
5	Fill gun	…	…	…
6	Switch on aeration	…	…	…
7	Put on breathing protection	…	…	…
8	Set spray gun	…	…	…
	Total time	…	…	…

DEFINE

Level 3:

Streamline of remaining internal activities

– Streamline the remaining internal activities by approaches for simplifying, eliminating and reducing.
– Reduce or eliminate the use of hand tools, and required nuts and srews.
– Use materials that help to prevent defects occurring directly at source.

| *Bayonet coupling* | *Quick clamp* | *Pneumatic screw driver* |

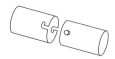

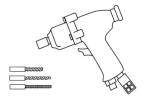

MEASURE

Level 4:

Eliminate adjustments and trial runs

– Eliminate intuition and estimates from adjustments and replace them by facts.
– Use visual control mechanisms to reduce adjustment times caused by inaccurate alignments, settings and measurements.

Colored marking of the target area

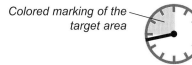

ANALYZE

⇒ **Tips**

• Always take into consideration when planning and carrying out these changes that time, technical and financial resources are limited.
• Use a value stream map in the preparation phase to identify constraints.

IMPROVE

CONTROL

Generic Pull System

🗀 Term
Generic Pull System, Flow Pull System

⏱ When
In the Improve Phase, generating solutions

◎ Goals
- Stabilize the process lead times by reducing the process WIP ("work in process").
- Increase process speed and thus flexibility as well.
- Optimize quality through earlier detection of defects.
- Generate more transparent process flows.

Example of Pull Systems

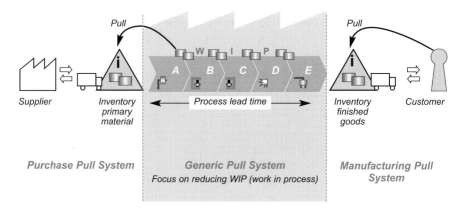

| Supplier | Inventory primary material | ← Process lead time → | Inventory finished goods | Customer |

| Purchase Pull System | Generic Pull System
Focus on reducing WIP (work in process) | Manufacturing Pull System |

▶▶ Steps
- Apply the 4-Step Methodology for calculating the WIP cap (WIP cap: arithmetically calculated upper limit for "work in process" within a defined sub-process):

214

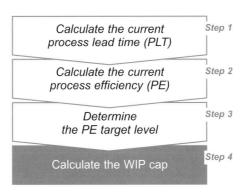

1. Calculate the current process lead time (PLT):
Determine the process lead time (time between a product entering the production process to its completion) according to Little's law.

Little's Law

$$PLT = \frac{\text{WIP [quantity]}}{\text{exit rate [quantity/t]}}$$

2. Calculate the process efficiency (PE):
Determine the process efficiency by taking into account the value-adding-time and the process lead time.

$$\text{Process efficiency} = \frac{\text{value-adding time [t]}}{\text{process lead time [t]}} \cdot 100\,[\%]$$

3. Determine the PE target level:
Define the target level of process efficiency based on the benchmark.
- For machining you find best practice PEs of up to 25 %, in assembly areas up to 80 %.
  Administrative processes reach a maximum of 50 %.
- If the current PE is much smaller than the best practice PE, target PE should be set at a realistic level, at least current PE + 50 % in the first step.

4. Calculate the WIP cap:

Calculate the WIP cap to define the maximal WIP level of a process. The interim buffers are to be lowered successively to match the possibilities of production (e.g. reducing unplanned idle times). In order to calculate the WIP cap again Little's Law is used. The target PLT in this equation is determined by the value added time divided through the target PE.

$$\text{WIP cap [quantity]} = \frac{\text{value-adding time [t]}}{\text{target PE}} \cdot \text{exit rate [quantity/t]}$$

Example of Guiding Principle for a Generic Pull System:
STARTS = EXITS

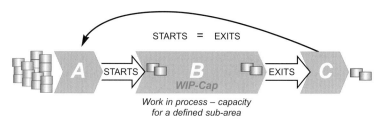

Work in process – capacity
for a defined sub-area

Replenishment Pull System

📁 **Term**
Replenishment Pull System

🕐 **When**
In the Improve Phase, generating solutions

◎ **Goals**
– Equalize supplier and consumer processes to prevent delivery con-
straints and provide the customer with a greater degree of flexibility.
– Generate a more up-to-date and transparent sales and production
planning.
– Reduce cost and effort put into re-planning.
– Create more room for flexible action when meeting short-term orders.

▶▶ **Steps**
– Replenish means to "fill up" and is used to position strategic stocks for:
raw materials, primary materials, procured parts, finished goods.

Example of Pull Systems

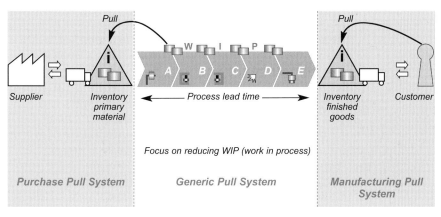

DEFINE MEASURE ANALYZE IMPROVE CONTROL

– The Replenishment Pull System is not based on forecasts but is rather triggered and steered by direct demand.

1. Test the prerequisites for deploying Replenishment Pull Systems:
   – The process lead time is greater than the lead time expected by the customer.
   – Production program remains constant.
   – Customer demand is relatively stable and varies only little.

2. Test the pull system capability:
   – *Demand flow:*
   Pull capable are only parts that vary little in terms of demand and can thus be accurately predicted. Use an XYZ analysis to classify parts:
   - Parts with constant demand (X-parts)
     → Primarily pull capable
   - Parts with fluctuating demand (Y-parts)
   - Parts with completely irregular demand (Z-parts)

	Demand	Forecast accuracy/ planning
X-parts	Constant (continuous), fluctuations rare	High
Y-parts	Stronger fluctuations (half continuous), mostly seasonal reasons	Moderate
Z-parts	Completely irregular demand (stochastic)	Low

   – *Product qualities:*
   Concentrate on products which are especially important for the company. A small number of parts often represent the largest proportion of demand. Use an ABC analysis:
   - **A-parts**
     Parts which are consumed in particularly great amounts and/ or their value-based demand is particularly high over a defined time period. Approx. 80 % of the total value of all parts account for approx. 10 % of the whole inventory:
     → Primarily pull capable.
   - **B-parts**
     Parts whose value-based demand moves in a middle range. Approx. 15 % of the total value accounts for approx. 20 % of the total inventory.

- **C-parts**
  Parts whose value-based demand is very low or which are only rarely deployed and/or are low-priced. Approx. 5% of the total value of all parts accounts for approx. 70% of the total inventory.

3. **Calculate the pull system parameters**
   Differentiating observations for finished goods (→ Manufacturing Pull System) and primary materials (→ Purchase Pull System):

Strategic Buffer for Primary Materials	Strategic Buffer for Finished Goods
Purchase Pull Systems	Manufacturing Pull Systems
• Demand	• Demand
• Supplier lead time	• Process lead time
• Order frequency	• Cycle time interval
• Safety stock	• Safety stock

Parameters used within the frame of a Manufacturing Pull System:
– *Demand*
  - Weekly or daily average customer need.
  - Based on historical or forecasted values.
  - Regular new calculations to capture changes in trends.
– *Process lead time*
  - Time between introducing a product into the manufacturing process and its completion as a finished good.
– *Cycle time interval*
  - Represents the time (days) according to which a specific part is manufactured again – is influenced by batch sizes and demand.
  - The cycle time interval depends on the parts, i.e. each part has its own lead time.
– *Safety stock*
  - Inventory that is required to compensate customer and manuacturing variation (e.g. demand fluctuations, production idle times, fluctuations in procuring materials).

DEFINE

MEASURE

ANALYZE

IMPROVE

CONTROL

Dimensioning Strategic Buffer Stocks in a Manufacturing Pull System

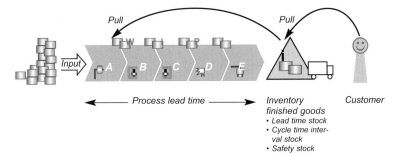

Process lead time — Inventory finished goods
• Lead time stock
• Cycle time inter-val stock
• Safety stock

Customer

Parameters used within the frame of a Purchase Pull System:
– *Demand*
- Weekly or daily average customer demand (production)
- Based on historical or forecasted values
- Regular new calculations to capture changes in trends
– *Supplier lead time*
Time between an order being placed with the supplier till receiving the ordered parts
– *Order frequency*
Represents the frequency (days) with which a specific part has to be ordered from the supplier
– *Safety stock*
Inventory that is required to compensate for production and supplier variation (e.g. idle times, delivery constraints, etc) as well as the service level.

2 Bin Replenishment Pull

A 2 Bin Replenishment Pull System is a simplified variant of the standardized replenishment pull system that uses two bins with products requiring restocking:
- Bin 1 contains enough of the product for a pre-calculated period; it is located directly at the workplace.
- When bin 1 is nearly empty, bin 2 is moved to the workplace while bin 1 is refilled.

For the 2 Bin Replenishment Pull System the same elements are basically used as for the standardized Replenishment Pull System.

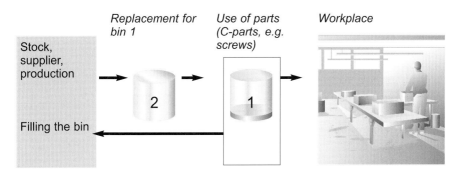

Tip
For further details determining the required amount of stock refer to relevant literature. This is necessary because of very different stock strategies and approaches in various branches.

Poka Yoke

📁 **Term**

Poka Yoke, mistake proofing or defect (error, mistake) avoidance

🕐 **When**

In the Improve phase, generating solutions

◎ **Goals**

– Apply preventive methods for avoiding defects directly at the source and response methods for the immediate detection of defects.
– Achieve 100 % defect avoidance.

▶▶ **Steps**

Preventive and reactive Poka Yoke approaches:

Preventive approach:
– Implement methods that *do not permit* the production of a defect.
– 100 % elimination of defects (zero defects).

Reactive approach of control/warning:
– Stop the process or signal the occurrence of a defect to the employee.
– Fix the defective part when a process step is incomplete.
– Stop the process when irregularities occur (makes sense if preventing the defect is too cost intensive).
– High probability of achieving the goal of zero defects.

Poka Yoke examination methods:
– *Traditional examination:*
  Divide into good parts and scraps or rework.

Examination Methods

Examination methods		
Traditional examination		• Divide into good parts and scrap/rework • Reduce the defective parts delivered to the customers • Does not prevent error production • Slow feedback via scrap/rework
Statistical examination		• System to reduce costs for examination • Does not prevent error production, does not ensure non-defective parts • Errors can be passed through due to examination of samples • Slow feedback via scrap/rework
Continuous examination		• Every process step controls the quality of the previous process • 100% of the parts are examined • Does not prevent error production • High effort/expenses of examination – efficient only for small amounts
Self-examination		• Every process step controls its own quality • Immediate feedback and corrective measures • Stops the further processing of a defective part • High effort/expenses of examination – 100% of the parts are examined
Complete examination		• Every process controls its own quality and that of its supplier • Problems are identified before the process step comes to an end • Immediate feedback and corrective measures • Stops the further processing of a defective part • High effort/expenses of examination – 100% of the parts are examined

DEFINE MEASURE ANALYZE IMPROVE CONTROL

DEFINE

MEASURE

ANALYZE

IMPROVE

CONTROL

Tip

The earlier the error is detected in the process the lower the costs for its elimination.

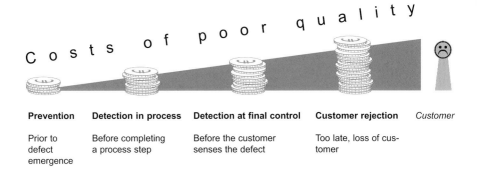

Prevention	**Detection in process**	**Detection at final control**	**Customer rejection**	*Customer*
Prior to defect emergence	Before completing a process step	Before the customer senses the defect	Too late, loss of customer	

Total Productive Maintenance (TPM)

📁 Terms
Total Productive Maintenance, Total Predictive Maintenance

🕐 When
In the Improve phase, generating solutions: When scheduled or unscheduled downtimes contribute to poorer process efficiency

◎ Goals
– Raise facility and equipment effectiveness to over 85% by eliminating sources of waste, e.g. downtimes, setup times, idle times, reduced takt speed, startup problems, and quality loss.
– Ensure that operations are running smoothly without unscheduled downtimes and that production is free of defects.
– Observe and optimize the interaction between work force, equipment, and work station.

▸▸ Steps

A. Analyze the current situation:
– Document the costs of maintenance and repairs (replacement parts and working hours).
– Determine the Overall Equipment Effectiveness (OEE) to find out the proportion in which the machine produces quality at a given takt rate.

B. Quick Check in order to restore equipment:
Inspect and clean machine, identify necessary repairs, and mark defects which need to be eliminated.
– Clean the machines and equipment
– During the cleaning process inspect everything
– Identify necessary repairs and mark areas that need repairing
– Document all necessary repairs and create a schedule
– Carry out repairs

C. Implement the concept for "preventive maintenance":
Structure maintenance to ensure a stable production process and to monitor the equipment with scheduled ("preventive") measures so that no unscheduled downtimes occur.

1. *Define the maintenance priorities:*
Identify those areas (equipment / or production areas) which occupy the maintenance department most in terms of breakdowns, replacement parts, etc. Introduce logbooks to record all incidents affecting the equipment.

2. *Create a stable basis for operations:*
Undertake a detailed analysis of weak points for parts and components susceptible to breakdown, using the logbooks and other relevant documents.

3. *Introduce the information, planning and steering system (IPS):*
Document and evaluate the specific information on the facilities and required maintenance activities. Computer-supported maintenance measures can be planned, steered and coordinated on this basis.

4. *Introduce process-related maintenance:*
Undertake regular inspection and maintenance of the facilities. Maintenance plans listing the tasks to be undertaken yearly, monthly or weekly help to coordinate these inspection and servicing measures.

5. *Optimize internal operations:*
Optimize existing internal maintenance sequences when carrying out maintenance measures. Possible optimization approaches:
   – Shorten the diagnosis of defects.
      → Analyzing breakdowns is often very time-consuming.
   – Optimize the storage of replacement parts.
      → Optimal storage directly influences the repair time.
   – Optimize the exchange of replacement parts.
      → Reduce the time needed to exchange parts.

6. *Secure sustainability – continually improve preventive maintenance program:*
   - Guarantee the early detection of problems by training employees in preventive and prognosis maintenance methods.
   - Install visual controls.
   - Implement 5 S.
   - Regularly control and improve machine performance.
     - Is the equipment that causes most problems identified?
     - Have all the weak points been effectively eliminated?
     - Can the IPS system be further improved?
     - Can the maintenance plans and standards be further improved?
     - How effective are the maintenance department's measures and workflows?
     - Can the repair and service times be further reduced?
     - What are the key TPM indicators showing?
       - Overall equipment effectiveness (OEE)
       - Mean time between failure (MTBF) and
       - Mean time to repair (MTTR)

⇨ Tips

- Machine operators must be instructed in the basic maintenance activities like cleaning, oiling / greasing, identifying damage, etc.
- Familiarity with and know-how of the equipment contributes to raising productivity and reducing downtimes.
- TPM is only successful when all employees are actively involved.

An example of a maintenance plan as part of a TPM system is given on the next page.

DEFINE

MEASURE

ANALYZE

IMPROVE

CONTROL

Example Maintenance Plan

Machine No				Machine Name	
Chart No				Manufacturer	
No	Machine parts to be lubricated		Lubricant	Quantity	Method	by
1	Pneumatic control panel	□	ESSO ZD5	50 ml	Orange oil can	PRD
2	Stock 1 and 2	△	SHELL T32	2 l	Blue tank	RS
3	Shaft	○	ESSO ZD5	0.5 l	Control oil level	PRD
4	Spindle	△	SHELL T16	1 l	Violet jerry can	RS
5	Gear unit	□	ESSO ZD5	10 ml	Control oil level	PRD
6	Tracks	△	SHELL T3	/	Green container	RS
7	Hinge joints	△	SHELL T11	/	Blue oil can	RS
8	Power unit 3	△	ESSO ZD5	0.5 l	Red jerry can	PRD
9	Power unit 4	△	SHELL T11	1.5 l	Blue oil can	PRD
10	Power unit 5	△	ESSO ZD5	1 l	Red jerry can	PRD

□ daily
○ weekly
△ monthly

RS = repairs & servicing	PRD = production	Creation date

Lean for Service

☐ Term

Lean for service, lean management in the service industry sector

◷ When

In the Improve Phase, generating solutions

◎ Goal

Transfer some lean methods and tools to administrative and service-oriented areas.

▶▶ Steps

Identify sources of waste in administrative areas with the aid of the "Seven Office Sins":

1. Unnecessary information transport
– Movement of documents from workplace to workplace
– Movement of documents between administration and production
– Passing through chains of authorization, hierarchies, and filing systems that are unnecessary

2. Information overflow
More information (e-mails, photocopies, memos, etc) than the customer, subsequent processes or the current project phase requires

3. Unnecessary ways
– Ways employees have to take when searching for documents
– Ways employees have to take when consulting colleagues located at different sites
– Ergonomic hurdles

4. Waiting times
Waiting for:
– Releases and / or decisions by superiors
– Files to be returned
– Orders to be handed on
– Technical warm-up times of office equipment

5. Unnecessary inventory
- Documents of finished projects
- Working tools and data sets never used
- Duplicate filing

6. Useless activities
- Reports, statistics and protocols nobody reads
- Repeated manually entered data
- Unnecessary photocopying

7. Errors
- Different media breaks in data formats
- Illegible faxes and notes
- Incomplete specifications

Increase process speed by reducing the WIP level in an administrative environment:
- Controlling the WIP level (documents, forms, notes, mails, voicemails, etc.) is the primary lever for increasing process speed in the administrative environment
- Determining a WIP upper limit (WIP cap) on the basis of Little's law ensures that the number of things (documents, forms, etc.) given in the respective working process is limited to this level
- The intake of the process is determined by processed documents leaving the process: A new document is only introduced to the process when a completed one can be passed on (starts = exists)

Important:
- Manage the process intake with a priority system
- This approach is for processes that are not directly customer-relevant – not for Point of Scale (POS)

Setup time reduction
Apply approaches for reducing setup times in an administrative and service-oriented environment:
- The method for setup reduction can always be applied when…
  - information must be tracked back to complete reports
  - required information is not available when needed
  - tasks have to be changed
  - tasks can be completed in "batches" for convenience

- All examples reveal sources of waste and hinder or prevent value-adding work
- Reducing setup times in the administrative area focuses on activities stopping the value-adding work process. Systematically identify reasons for such breakdowns and develop solutions
- Simplify necessary activities disrupting the process. For example, use electronic notes and reminders to accelerate complex working steps

Example of Setup Time Reduction

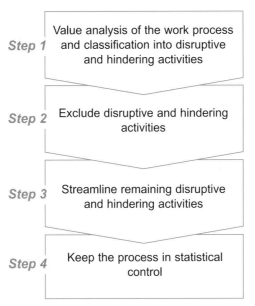

Step 1 — Value analysis of the work process and classification into disruptive and hindering activities

Step 2 — Exclude disruptive and hindering activities

Step 3 — Streamline remaining disruptive and hindering activities

Step 4 — Keep the process in statistical control

Brainstorming

☐ **Term**
Brainstorming

🕐 **When**
Project selection, in the Analyze and Improve Phases

◎ **Goal**
Generate and collect ideas.

▶▶ **Steps**
1. Determine the rules for the brainstorming session with the team.
2. Identify and write down the topics and the question.
3. Develop ideas.
4. Collect ideas.
5. Explain ideas and structure or cluster them *(see affinity matrix)*.
6. Build on single ideas through a new brainstorming.

Facilitating a brainstorming session
How a brainstorming session is facilitated is decisive for its success. A facilitator always leads the session. There are different ways for collecting the ideas:
– Flip chart:
The facilitator collects the ideas and writes them on the chart.
– Pin board (1):
The facilitator collects the ideas, writes them down and pins them randomly on the board. Clustering is undertaken later in group work.
– Pin board (2):
Each participant writes down his ideas and structures them around already existing topics (forming clusters).
Which form of facilitation is chosen depends on the facilitator and team.

Brainstorming rules
– Listen to the contributions of others – do not interrupt
– Each proposal counts
– All participants participate actively

232

- Do not use any "killer" phrases
- Place quantity before quality
- No concrete discussions on content and no explanations
- Everything is noted down.

⇨ **Tips**

- Suitable timeframe: 5-10 minutes.
- Write down the brainstorming rules and place them in the room so that everyone can read them.

Example of Brainstorming

DEFINE

MEASURE

ANALYZE

IMPROVE

CONTROL

Anti-Solution Brainstorming

☐ **Term**
Anti-solution brainstorming

🕐 **When**
In the Improve Phase

◎ **Goals**
– Collect ideas for identifying solutions by considering, "What could make the situation worse?"
– Resolve blockages hampering the identification of solutions.

▶▶ **Steps**
1. Establish rules
2. Identify and write down the topics, "What could make the situation worse?"
3. Develop ideas
4. Collect ideas
5. Explain the ideas and structure or cluster them
6. Convert ideas into proposals for improvement
7. Go further into single ideas through a new brainstorming

Apply the brainstorming rules for this.

⇨ **Tips**
• Use red tags for anti-solutions and then green tags for positive solutions.
• After generating anti-solutions carry out another brainstorming to derive positive solutions without much discussion.

Example of Anti-Solution Brainstorming

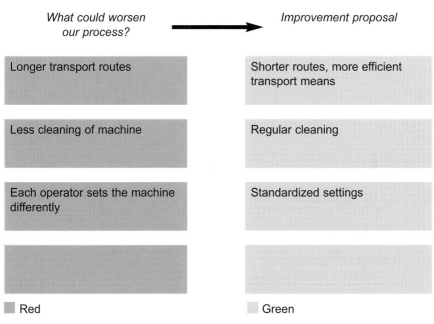

What could worsen our process? → Improvement proposal

What could worsen our process? (Red)	Improvement proposal (Green)
Longer transport routes	Shorter routes, more efficient transport means
Less cleaning of machine	Regular cleaning
Each operator sets the machine differently	Standardized settings

Red

Green

Brain Writing

⬚ **Term**

Brain writing

🕐 **When**

Project selection, in the Analyze and Improve Phases

◎ **Goals**

– Develop ideas in a team in a relaxed atmosphere.
– Generate unusual relationships between and combinations of ideas.

▶▶ **Steps**

Classical brain writing

1. Determine the topic together
2. Each member gets a DIN A4 sheet of paper
3. Each member notes down an idea for solving the problem
4. Each member passes on the sheet to his or her neighbor in a clockwise direction (everyone at the same time)
5. Consider the predecessor's idea, elaborate on it or develop a completely new one
6. Pass on the sheet again.
7. Collect all the sheets at the end of a set time
8. Fix the sheets to a board and explain the contents
9. Summarize the proposals on a flip chart or cards

Brain writing 6-3-5

Brain writing 6-3-5 follows the classical model. The term stands for the idea that 6 persons write down and pass on 3 ideas in 5 minutes.

Idea card method

This method is another variation of classical brain writing. Here the ideas are collected on cards or post-it notes. The advantage is that there is no need to rewrite the ideas later.

Brain writing pool
Here the ideas are not passed on clockwise systematically, but are collected in the middle of the table. Each team member can draw one or more ideas from the pool and develop it further.

Notebook method
Instead of collecting the ideas during a session, each team member can note down his own ideas irrespective of time and place. The ideas are passed on to other team members through e-mail. After a set period they are collected and discussed at a team meeting. A typical timeframe for this kind of brain writing is 2 to 4 weeks.

⇨ Tips
- Visualize and present the developed solutions so that they are easily visible.
- Begin with a topic and collect all the formulated ideas – then continue with the next topic on the agenda. Mark all ideas formulated.
- The ideas can be improved with the team so that they become more comprehensible.

Illustration Brain Writing
Example1: brain writing 6-3-5

Example 2: notebook method

SCAMPER

📁 **Term**
SCAMPER

🕐 **When**
In each phase when applying creativity techniques

◎ **Goals**
- Support creativity when identifying solutions.
- Provide a structure for activities when developing solution ideas.

▶▶ **Steps**
The SCAMPER checklist is a valuable instrument that supports the creativity techniques presented above.

Substitute	What can be substituted by what? Can the process be designed differently? Are there elements from other countries or times?
Combine	What can be combined with something else? Can x be connected to other ideas, subdivided into modules, and transformed into a different image?
Adapt	How can ... be adapted? Can parallels be identified? Can we understand it?
Modify	How can ... be changed (maximized, minimized)? – meaning, color, movement, size, form, etc. – enlarge something, add something, increase the frequency – reduce something, remove something, lower the frequency
Put to other uses	How can ... be put to a different use? Does it have other possible uses? Can x be deployed elsewhere?

Eliminate / erase	How can ... be eliminated or erased? Is x really necessary?
Reverse / rearrange	What happens when ...x is reversed or rearranged? Can the sequence be changed? Can the idea be depicted back-to-front? Can the points be exchanged?

⇨ **Tip**

The best approach is to construct a matrix plotting the ideas and process steps of the current process and pose the SCAMPER questions for each process step or idea.

Example of SCAMPER

	S	C	A	M	P	E	R
Process step 1 and / or idea 1							
Process step 2 and / or idea 2							
Process step 3 and / or idea 3							
Etc.							

DEFINE

MEASURE

ANALYZE

IMPROVE

CONTROL

Affinity Diagram

📁 **Term**
Affinity diagram, clustering

🕐 **When**
While applying creativity techniques

◎ **Goal**
Cluster and summarize ideas to understand the core statements.

▶▶ **Steps**
1. Sort and structure the ideas into topics
2. Give each group of ideas a concise heading

⇥ **Tips**
- Always look for the logical connection when sorting the ideas. If the idea is being moved from one group to another, then write it down again and assign it to both groups.
- Some cards can well stand alone. They can be just as important as those ideas which can be grouped instantly.

Example of an Affinity Diagram

Topic		
Heading 1	*Heading 2*	*Heading 3*
Idea	Idea	Idea
Idea	Idea	Idea
Idea	Idea	Idea

Must Criteria

☐ **Term**
Must criteria

🕐 **When**
In the Improve Phase, when beginning to select solutions

◎ **Goal**
Review the generated solutions to see if they can be implemented with respect to really relevant solutions.

▶▶ **Steps**
Closely examine every possible solution based on must criteria, i.e. criteria which have to be met unconditionally. Examples of such criteria are
– legal regulations,
– safety regulations,
– fulfilling customer requirements,
– company strategy and philosophy,
– internal company working agreements,
– norms and standards,
– ecological requirements.

Reject the solution if it cannot meet these requirements.

⇨ **Tip**
Make the solutions to be removed clearly visible on the board and then include them in the project documentation.

An example is given on the following page.

DEFINE

Example of Must Criteria

Criteria list	Criteria not fulfilled	Criteria fulfilled
Regulation 1		
Regulation 2		
Company strategy		
Company working agreements		
Norm 1		
Norm 2		

MEASURE

ANALYZE

IMPROVE

CONTROL

Effort-Benefit Matrix

📁 **Term**
Effort-benefit matrix, profitability matrix

🕐 **When**
In the Improve phase, after examining the must criteria

◎ **Goals**
- Evaluate all the possible solutions in terms of effort and benefit.
- Select the solutions possessing the most favorable effort-benefit ratio.

▶▶ **Steps**
1. Review each solution as to the effort demanded and the benefits to be gained. The team undertakes the evaluation
2. Enter the solutions into a matrix
3. Reject solutions with high effort and little benefit
4. Prioritize solutions involving little effort but generating great benefit for further consideration

⇨ **Tip**
Write down the assumptions used for sorting the proposed solutions – this keeps everything transparent and verifiable.

Example of an Effort-Benefit Matrix

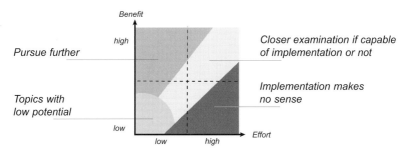

243

DEFINE

MEASURE

ANALYZE

IMPROVE

CONTROL

N/3 Method

📁 **Term**
N/3 method, N over 3 method

🕐 **When**
In the Improve Phase after examining the effort benefit relation if there are several alternative solutions which are mutually exclusive

◎ **Goal**
Reduce the number of alternative solutions by removing the least preferable ones.

▶▶ **Steps**
1. Each member gets adhesive dots. The number handed out is to be one-third of the proposals for discussion
2. The dots are handed out randomly
3. The proposed solutions gaining the most dots (points) remain in the running. Repeat until the desired reduction is achieved
4. Discussion is allowed between the voting steps to form a consensus (facilitator needed!)

⇒ **Tip**
After completing the voting recheck together if the rejected alternatives really deserve to be discarded!
Attention: This method only makes sense when genuine alternatives exist. Do not employ the method when the solutions can be implemented in combination with one another and are financially feasible!

Example of the N/3 method
Example of car dealer: proposed solutions

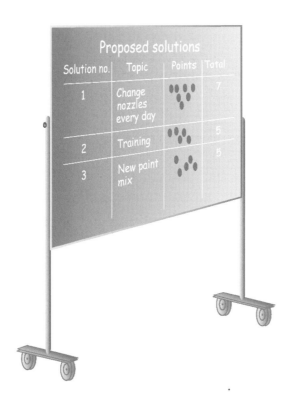

Nominal Group Technique

📁 **Term**

Nominal group technique

🕐 **When**

Project selection, Improve when selecting alternative solutions and there are no more than 12 proposals

◎ **Goals**

– Prioritize topics, problems, and the alternative solutions.
– Evaluate a manageable number of alternative solutions through a team of experts.

▶▶ **Steps**

1. List the remaining solutions and enter them into a table. Eliminate all ambiguities. Make sure there is general agreement on the formulations
2. Assign a letter to each solution
3. Each team member ranks the solutions. The highest-ranked solution receives the highest number of points, corresponding to the number of solutions
4. Discuss outlier evaluations
5. Add up the values. The solution with the highest total value is the one selected by the group

⇨ **Tips**

- Here, as well, only evaluate solution alternatives, which cannot be implemented at the same time.
- If two or more solutions achieve the same score discuss where the differences in the evaluation are. It is possible that team members understand the solution differently.

Example of Nominal Group Technique
Example: car dealer
Question: which of the listed solutions is to be pursued further?

Topic / solutions	Person A	Person B	Person C	Sum
A New paint supplier	3	5	4	12
B Training	7	3	3	13
C New mixing scales	4	2	2	8
D New undercoat	5	6	6	17
E New employees	2	4	1	7
F New nozzles	6	7	7	20
G Remodel paint box	1	1	5	7

DEFINE

MEASURE

ANALYZE

IMPROVE

CONTROL

DEFINE

MEASURE

ANALYZE

IMPROVE

CONTROL

Prioritization Matrix

☐ Term
Prioritization matrix, criteria-based selection, criteria-based ranking

⊘ When
Project selection, in the Improve Phase when selecting from alternative solutions and there are no more than 12 proposals

◎ Goals
- Systematically narrow the options by using criteria to compare, assess and select the most promising possibilities.
- Evaluate a manageable number of solutions using weighted criteria.

▶▶ Steps
1. Draw up a definitive list of solutions. Make sure they are formulated clearly and succinctly
2. Draw up a list of criteria. The team must agree on the criteria
3. Assess and weight the criteria
4. Evaluate the solutions using the weighted criteria
5. Add up the scores for each solution and discuss the results

⇨ Tip
The Sponsor or a neutral person should weight the criteria.

Example of a Prioritization Matrix

		Possible solutions			
		Solution A		Solution B	
Criteria	*Weighting*	*Points*	*Weighted Points*	*Points*	*Weighted Points*
1. Integrate other depts. and persons into the changes	5	10	50	5	25
2. Reversibility of the measure	6	10	60	2	12
3. Costs and effort needed for imple-- mentation	10	5	50	10	100
4. Significance for the success of the project	8	3	24	10	80
5. Risk of the process deteriorating	2	10	20	5	10
	Total	38	204	32	227

Solution B is selected

DEFINE

MEASURE

ANALYZE

IMPROVE

CONTROL

Cost-Benefit Analysis

📁 **Term**
Cost-benefit analysis

🕐 **When**
In the Improve Phase when selecting the solutions

◎ **Goal**
Evaluate the selected solutions or compare a smaller number of solutions.

▶▶ **Steps**
– The 12 months prior to project start form the basis for the calculations
– The 12 months after implementing improvements are the observation period.
– Include implementation costs on the cost side
– Do not formulate a narrow concept of benefit: besides the effect on profits, take into consideration increases in productivity and other benefits which are not directly calculable.
– Include the usual company calculations in the cost-benefit analysis.
– The result of the selected project represents the net benefit generated by the executed project.

⇒ **Tip**
Consult an expert from the controlling department.

Example of a cost-benefit analysis

Example: criteria-based selection for the car dealer / paint workshop

	Year 0 (12 months prior to project)	Year 1 (12 months after project)
1. Turnover		
2. Costs		
2.1. Personnel costs (incl. additional expenses)		
2.2. Production materials expenses		
2.3. Scrap and rework costs		
2.4. Maintenance costs		
2.5. Storage costs		
2.6. Other costs		
3. Exceptional expenses / implementation costs		
3.1. Machines / equipment		
3.2. Training		
3.3. Other implementation costs		
4. Result		

DEFINE

MEASURE

ANALYZE

IMPROVE

CONTROL

DEFINE

MEASURE

ANALYZE

IMPROVE

CONTROL

Should-be Process Map

☐ Term
Should-be process map, target process map, future process map

☽ When
Improve phase after selecting the suitable solutions, planning the implementation

◎ Goals
- Depict the should-be process like it should be for implementing the chosen solutions
- All employees understand the effects of the improvements on the workflow
- Create the basis for the new workplace layout, documentation and working instructions

▶▶ Steps

Step 1
Choose the same form of mapping a process like in the Analyze phase (swim-lane, value stream map, …).

Step 2
Describe the future actions. The following subjects should be considered:
- The process represents the real value stream following the customer requirements.
- The number of process steps and therefore also the handovers are minimized.
- Plan with the target to reduce non-value-adding activities (rework, transport, …) and focus on value-adding ones. The effect is a better process efficiency.
- The total lead time of the process should be reduced.
- The process is balanced: Bottlenecks and constraints are compensated by eliminating non-value-adding activities and tasks are distributed in an equal way following the takt time.

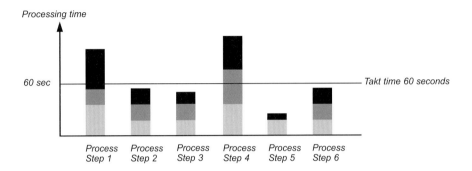

The individual process steps are not balanced.

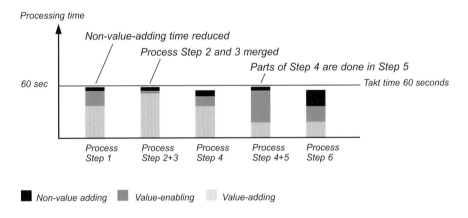

- Use "Pull" instead of "Push" in order to stabilize and reduce the WIP so that the total process lead time is also reduced.
- Defect source avoidance is needed considering Poka Yoke.
- The distances and time needed between the individual steps are reduced by improving the process flow.

Step 3
Identify the (new) functions or persons involved in the process.

Tip
Focus on those parts of the should-be process that are changed in future.

DEFINE

MEASURE

ANALYZE

IMPROVE

CONTROL

DEFINE

MEASURE

ANALYZE

IMPROVE

CONTROL

Activities Planning

☐ Terms
Activities planning, work packages

☉ When
In the Improve Phase, when planning implementation

◎ Goal
Define the work packages for all of the activities necessary for the successful implementation.

▶▶ Steps
1. List the selected solutions.
2. Identify the measures necessary for implementing the solutions.
3. Wrap up into work packages, e.g. "communication".
4. Distribute the tasks to those mainly responsible for their execution.
5. Set the start and end dates or the milestones for the work packages.
6. Integrate the Process Owner.

⇨ Tips
- Develop a change management strategy and in particular, a communication plan before launching implementation.
- Describe in detail the work packages for implementing the solutions. This prevents the risk that the solutions are implemented differently to how the team understood the tasks.

Example of Work Package

Work packages	Start - finish	Responsible
1. Should-be process	9/1/ - 12/31/	Mr. Goldberg
1.1 Document should-be process	9/18/ - 10/13/	
1.2 Draw up working instructions	9/18/ - 10/13/	
1.3 Implement should-be process	12/1/ - 12/31/	
2. Training measures	10/16/ - 12/31.	Ms. Vetter
2.1 Plan training measures	10/16/ - 10/31/	
2.2 Invite employees	10/16/ - 11/13/	
2.3 Conduct training	11/27/ - 12/31/	
3. Communication	9/1/ - 12/31/	Mr. Mayer
3.1 Draw up communication concept	9/1/ - 10/13/	
3.2 Implement communication concept	10/16/ - 12/31/	

DEFINE

MEASURE

ANALYZE

IMPROVE

CONTROL

Activities Plan and Schedule, Gantt Diagram

Terms

Gantt diagram, activities plan and schedule, action plan, Measure plan, implementation plan

When

In the Improve Phase when planning implementation

Goal

Set and depict all the activities, responsibilities and dates relevant for the implementation.

Steps

1. Break down the work packages and determine the activities in detail.
2. Set the start and end dates for each activity.
3. Also set dates (start-end) and responsibilities for implementation.
4. If necessary, add further details, such as implementation status, effort / benefit, etc.

Tip

- Always compare the implementation set in the plan with the respective current status.
- Always enter the target and current course of the activities. Plans that are optimized later lead to a loss of control over the implementation.
- Software packages like MS Project® support the presentation of the Gantt Diagram.

Example of a Gantt Diagram

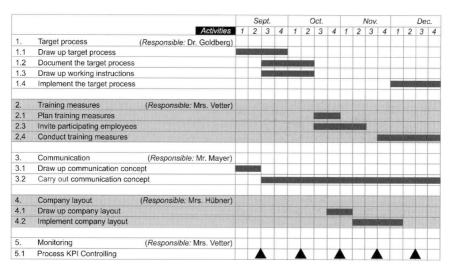

	Activities		Sept.				Oct.				Nov.				Dec.			
			1	2	3	4	1	2	3	4	1	2	3	4	1	2	3	4
1.	Target process *(Responsible:* Dr. Goldberg)																		
1.1	Draw up target process			▬	▬														
1.2	Document the target process					▬	▬	▬											
1.3	Draw up working instructions					▬	▬	▬											
1.4	Implement the target process															▬	▬	▬	▬
2.	Training measures *(Responsible:* Mrs. Vetter)																		
2.1	Plan training measures								▬										
2.3	Invite participating employees									▬	▬								
2,4	Conduct training measures														▬	▬	▬	▬	▬
3.	Communication *(Responsible:* Mr. Mayer)																		
3.1	Draw up communication concept			▬															
3.2	Carry out communication concept																		
4.	Company layout *(Responsible:* Mrs. Hübner)																		
4.1	Draw up company layout									▬									
4.2	Implement company layout												▬	▬	▬				
5.	Monitoring *(Responsible:* Mrs. Vetter)																		
5.1	Process KPI Controlling			▲			▲			▲			▲			▲			

DEFINE

MEASURE

ANALYZE

IMPROVE

CONTROL

Network Plan

☐ **Term**
Network plan

🕓 **When**
In the Improve Phase when planning implementation

◎ **Goal**
Visualize the work packages, their length of time, and their interdependency.

▶▶ **Steps**
Structure the work packages into a logical sequence.
Parallel steps are possible.

⇨ **Tips**
- Use the network plan when planning complex work flows before drawing up the schedule.
- Use post-it® notes on a pin board to draw up the network plan, after the brainstorming of the necessary activities.

Examples of Network Plans
1. Network plan

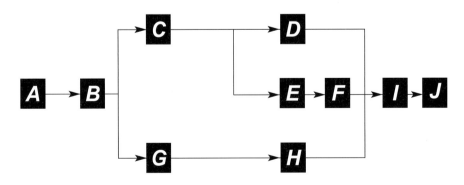

258

2. Network plan: the critical path

The critical path is the route through the project network that identifies the shortest period of time in which the project can be completed.

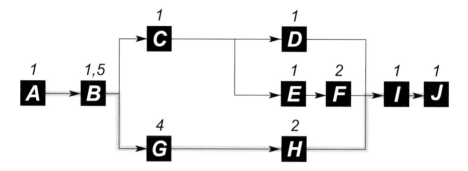

Activity	Description	Duration	Earliest		Latest		Delay
			Begin	End	Begin	End	
A	Draw up summary report for purchasing	1 Week	CW 10	CW 11	CW 10	CW 11	
B		...					
C		...					
D		...					
E		...					
F		...					
G		...					
H		...					
I		...					
J		...					

DEFINE

MEASURE

ANALYZE

IMPROVE

CONTROL

Risk Analysis

📁 **Term**
Risk analysis

🕐 **When**
Improve, when planning implementation and the action plan is certain

◎ **Goal**
Anticipate possible risks.

▶▶ **Steps**
1. Formulate remaining risks (after implementing the work packages).
2. Evaluate risks as to their impact.
3. If necessary, extend the activities plan to limit the impact, or better still to eliminate the risk.
4. Determine a reaction plan when minimizing a risk demands too much effort.

⇨ **Tips**
- An FMEA is a very helpful instrument for identifying and analyzing potential defects in the new process.
- The elaboration of a reaction plan serves as a basis for the Control Phase.

The FMEA was already explained in the Analyze Phase.

Budget and Resource Planning

📁 **Term**
Budget and resource planning

🕐 **When**
In the Improve Phase when planning the implementation

◎ **Goals**
– Identify the required budget and resources needs.
– Secure their availability.
– Plan and control an efficient deployment.

▶▶ **Steps**
1. The cost-benefit analysis is the starting point for planning budget and resources.
2. The project leader is responsible.

⇒ **Tip**
Work closely with the Sponsor when planning the budget.

Example of Planning

	Topic	Employees/days	KEUR
1.	Training		
1.1.	5 persons dept. A	$5 \cdot 3 = 15$	
1.2.	3 persons dept. B	$3 \cdot 2 = 6$	
1.3.	Trainer (internal)	3	
1.4.	Trainer (external)		5
2.	Materials costs		
2.1.	Equipment 1		35
2.2.	Equipment 2		4
2.3.	Equipment 3 (remodel)		10

DEFINE

MEASURE

ANALYZE

IMPROVE

CONTROL

Pilot Program

☐ **Term**

Pilot program, piloting

🕓 **When**

In the Improve Phase when planning implementation

◎ **Goals**

- Confirm expectations.
- Verify savings potential.
- Limit risks.
- Detect weaknesses.
- Gain a better understanding of impacts.
- Test acceptance.
- Gain relevant experience for the implementation.
- Optimize the solutions.
- Achieve a quicker implementation of sub-solutions.

▶▶ **Steps**

When do you launch a pilot program?

- If the changes to be implemented are extensive.
- If the solutions could trigger far-reaching, unpredictable consequences.
- If implementing the solutions is extremely cost intensive.
- If changes cannot be reversed easily.

Preparation

- Select a suitable area for piloting.
- Reach agreement with management on the selected area.
- Form a steering committee with managers for the pilot program.
- Develop implementation plans for the pilot program.
- Inform all those involved – gain the confidence of and integrate employees.

262

DEFINE

MEASURE

ANALYZE

IMPROVE

CONTROL

Execution
- Train the involved employees.
  - Each of the involved employees must understand their respective tasks and realize the importance of the pilot program.
  - Adjust the pilot program if necessary.
- Implement the pilot program and document the results.
  - Active participation and interest is imperative to ensure success. Undertake adjustments if necessary.
  - Make sure that feedback on the results is sent to employees, the steering committee, the project team, and management.
- Carry out briefings and reviews and undertake required adjustments.
  - Results are to be documented and presented in writing: Problems and solutions during the pilot.
- If the pilot proves successful consider extending it to another problem area.

⇨ **Tip**

If it is possible, carry out a pilot program – piloting reduces risks.

Example of a Deming Wheel

The Deming wheel, also known as the PDCA method, is especially suited for carrying out a pilot.

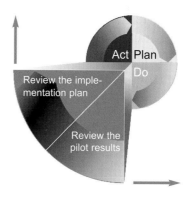

Adjustments can be made after reviewing the pilot results and the implementation plan.

Roll Out

☐ Term
Roll out, productive launch, implementation

☉ When
Phase Closure Improve

◎ Goals
– Implement the project results.
– Transfer the pilot results to the whole project.

▸▸ Steps
1. Complete pilot program.
2. Implement measures according to the action plan.
3. Use the PDCA method when problems arise.

⇨ Tip
The direct control / steering by the management as well as its support are absolutely necessary.

Example
Roll out planning

Phase	Dept.	Duration	Start	Completed	Delays	Measure
1	Dept. 1	4 weeks	CW 5	CW 9		
	Dept. 2	3 weeks	CW 5	CW 8		
2	Dept. 3	4 weeks	CW 10	CW 14		
3	Dept. 4-8	4 weeks	CW 15	CW 19		

Checklist for the Improve Phase

Solutions

Possible solutions are generated. ☑

Must and can criteria are defined. ☑

The best solutions are selected based on the criteria. ☑

The best solutions are evaluated based on the effort-benefit relation. ☑

A cost-benefit analysis is carried out for the selected best solutions. ☑

Implementation Plan

The should-be process is precisely defined. ☑

The activities, schedule and resource planning is completed, trainings and, where necessary, audit plans are taken into consideration. ☑

The persons responsible for implementation are identified. ☑

The possible risks were identified and quantified. ☑

Pilot

The possibilities of testing (piloting) the best solutions were evaluated. ☑

If necessary, a pilot program was carried out. The pilot results are transferred to the whole project area. ☑

Project Charter

The project goal and scope are reviewed and adjusted if necessary. ☑

The expected net benefit is reviewed and adjusted if necessary. ☑

Improve

Carry out the Gate Review. ☑

DEFINE

MEASURE

ANALYZE

IMPROVE

CONTROL

Six Sigma⁺Lean
Toolset

CONTROL

DEFINE

MEASURE

ANALYZE

IMPROVE

CONTROL

Phase 5: Control

Goals

- Control the optimized process using the essential measurements.
- Secure the project's sustainable and long-term success.

Steps

- Document the optimized process (should-be process) and relevant working instructions and procedures.
- Select the essential measurements required to maintain control of the process.
- Develop a reaction plan.
- Develop and implement a process management consisting of the should-be process, control measurements, and the reaction plan.
- Hand over the project results to the Process Owner.
- Monitor the control measurements.
- Review the actual benefit of the project.

Tools

- **Process Documentation**

- **Monitoring / Control Charts**

- **Reaction Plan / Process Management Diagram**

Should-be Process

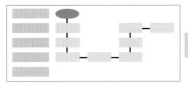

Documentation

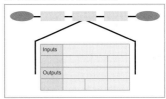

Monitoring / Control Charts

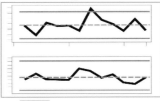

Reaction Plan

Documentation	Monitoring	Reaction Plan

Gate Review

Process Documentation

☐ Term
Process documentation, standardization

☉ When
In the Control phase, when a project is completed

◎ Goals
- Ensure that the improvements are standardized and institutionalized.
- Secure the communication of the process, i.e. that others can access it.
- Process documentation covers the entire process flow by taking into consideration the responsibilities, the working methods, and interfaces beneath the process level.

▶▶ Steps
- Document the procedural instructions.
- Audit the procedural instructions.
- Setup the work stations in line with procedural instructions.
- Train employees.
- Implement the procedural instructions.

⇨ Tips
- Observe working procedures in practice (inform employees beforehand)!
- Specifically ask the employees about the working procedures. Depict the procedure from the employees' viewpoint!
- Possible questions: "What difficulties do you have with the procedural instructions?" "How can we make work easier and still achieve the required results?"
- Draw up procedural instructions for only really important things – the more paper there is, the less it is read/used.

Example of Documentation

Procedural instructions / sample

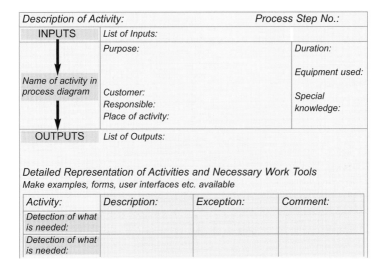

Description of Activity:		Process Step No.:	
INPUTS	List of Inputs:		
	Purpose:		Duration:
Name of activity in process diagram			Equipment used:
	Customer: Responsible: Place of activity:		Special knowledge:
OUTPUTS	List of Outputs:		

Detailed Representation of Activities and Necessary Work Tools
Make examples, forms, user interfaces etc. available

Activity:	Description:	Exception:	Comment:
Detection of what is needed:			
Detection of what is needed:			

Connection between process diagram and procedural instructions

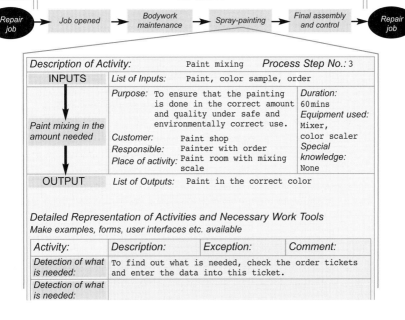

Description of Activity:	Paint mixing	Process Step No.: 3	
INPUTS	List of Inputs: Paint, color sample, order		
	Purpose: To ensure that the painting is done in the correct amount and quality under safe and environmentally correct use.		Duration: 60 mins
Paint mixing in the amount needed			Equipment used: Mixer, color scaler
	Customer: Paint shop Responsible: Painter with order Place of activity: Paint room with mixing scale		Special knowledge: None
OUTPUT	List of Outputs: Paint in the correct color		

Detailed Representation of Activities and Necessary Work Tools
Make examples, forms, user interfaces etc. available

Activity:	Description:	Exception:	Comment:
Detection of what is needed:	To find out what is needed, check the order tickets and enter the data into this ticket.		
Detection of what is needed:			

DEFINE　MEASURE　ANALYZE　IMPROVE　CONTROL

Visual Process Monitoring and Control

🗀 Terms
Visual Process Control, visual process monitoring

🕑 When
In the Control Phase the sustainability of the performance increase can be ensured by visual process control

◎ Goals
- Inform about the day-to-day performance at a glance.
- Enable direct feedback to the employees.
- Prioritize tasks.
- Transparency over the workflow.
- Recognize deviations from standards in an easy way.
- Ensure that safety, health, environmental and cleanliness concerns are being met.

▶▶ Steps
The steps depend on the different types of visual process monitoring and control.

1. Production Survey Boards / Andon Boards
- Production Survey Boards monitor the results of a process and allow us to judge if they are meeting customer needs.
- They should at least cover the following three core information:
  - the work performance in detail
  - the actual target equipment speed
  - the target speed

2. Production / Process Boards
- These boards focus on providing information on improvement projects or current process management.
- They should contain the following work station-relevant information:
  - Individual working operations within the process
  - Actual work performance in comparison to the targeted work performance (productivity rate, lead time, takt rate, cumulated

272

DEFINE

MEASURE

ANALYZE

IMPROVE

CONTROL

number of units produced, deliveries on time, idle time of machines [unplanned maintenance], etc.)
- Amount of WIP and the value of the WIP in Euros
- Unsolved problems divided into such problems which the working team can solve itself, and such problems which require the help of an expert (engineer, electrician etc.) or a person with a higher area of authority.

3. Personnel Performance and Training Boards
This board provides a list of all employees and helps to determine the employee's training need
- Status of the employees' skills
- Areas where they need further training.
- Helps to determine the priorities with respect to further training

4. 5 S or Kaizen Boards
They indicate the status of 5 S or Kaizen actions:
- Standardization checklists
- Spider web diagram for results of a 5 S check
- Action plan for improvement
- Before / after implementation photos
- Visualize what item has to be placed where (set in order)

Depicting the 5 S-Status

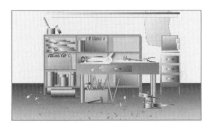

Example:
Before implementation photo

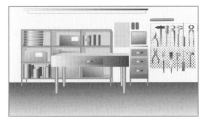

Example:
After implementation photo

Control Charts

📁 **Term**

Control charts, Shewart charts

🕐 **When**

Measure, Analyze and Control Phases, process monitoring

◎ **Goals**

– Process Monitoring; recognize and pursue process spreads.
– Find out if the process is stable and under control.
– Identify common and special causes.
– Set out the tools for steering the process.

▶▶ **Steps**

1. Determine the sample strategy and size

– Take samples for control charts. The correct sampling strategy is important.
– A sample strategy for control charts contains both its size as well as the frequency with which the sample is taken. This means: always take a sample of a specific size at a set point in time or after a specific number of parts.
– In terms of timing, always select the samples so that they deliver the most meaningful statement on how the process is developing. If the wrong point in time is selected, e.g. when raw materials are being changed, then it is very likely that a decisive swing factor emerges, one that, however, provides little meaningful information.

⇨ **Tips**

• Take time and costs into account when selecting the strategy.
• If possible, take samples under the same conditions (e.g. the same machine).

Forming Subgroups

- Gaining a meaningful and effective statement from the Control charts depends on the quality of the sample and the quality of the subgroups.

- When forming subgroups make sure that …
  - they deliver the best possible information about the process, and
  - they depict the variation of the output or input in its entirety, because the entire variation (both within a subgroup and between subgroups) determines the limits for the Control chart.

- The subgroups should be formed rationally. There are two approaches for forming rational subgroups:
  - The units are produced from the sample simultaneously (or in due course) (see remarks on sample size and frequency).
  - The sample is representative for all units produced since the last sample was taken. Essentially this means a random sample from all produced units since the last sample was taken. This approach (representative sample) is strongly recommended when there is reason to assume that the process was not under control for a specific period of time but that statistical control has since been reestablished. In this case, the first method would not be sufficiently effective to detect this shift. However, caution is needed when interpreting Control charts in this context: if the process has shifted several times within this time interval this can lead to a considerable increase in the variation of the sample. This means in turn that the control limits are wider. In principle every process can be interpreted as under control if the intervals between the samples are big enough.

Rational Subgroups

The idea behind rational subgroups can be illustrated with an Xbar-R chart. To explain this we will focus on identifying the shift of the mean value: forming rational subgroups means that they are selected in such a way that, given the existence of special causes, the probability of differences between the subgroups is maximized, and concurrently, that the probability of differences within the subgroup is minimized due to these special causes.

DEFINE

MEASURE

ANALYZE

IMPROVE

CONTROL

⇨ **Tips**
- The factors of time and costs are to be considered when deriving the sample strategy and determining the sample size.
- Take samples under the same conditions whenever possible (e.g. same work station, machine).
- When forming rational subgroups it may make sense to formulate separate control charts for different stratification factors (e.g. work station / machine, operator, work shift).

2. **Select the suitable control chart depending upon data type and sample size**

Continuous and discrete data

- *Continuous data*
  - Two graphs are drawn up for control charts with continuous data material: in the first, the mean value or the single values per group are entered; in the second, the range or standard deviation of each subgroup.
  - The sample size for continuous data is usually between four to six measurements.
  - Control limits of ±3s are normally used.
  - 99.73% of data thus lie within these limits (given normal distribution).

- *Discrete data*
  - One graph is drawn up for discrete data material in which one can enter: for example, the proportion or number of defective parts, the number of defects or the defects per unit of each subgroup.

Data type		Sample size (subgroup)	Control chart
Continuous data		1	IMR-chart
		< 10 (usually 3 - 5); constant	Xbar-R-chart
		> 10 and / or variable	Xbar-S-chart
Discrete data	Defects per unit	Constant (usually > 50); no. of defects > 5	c-chart
		Variable (usually > 50); no. of defects > 5	u-chart
	Defective units	Constant (usually > 50)	np-chart
		Variable (usually > 50)	p-chart

3. **Collect data, pay attention to the:**
   - Data collection plan
   - Operational definition
   - Measurement system analysis if required

4. **Calculate the statistics and the control limits:**
   - Several statistics programs support the automatic generation of control charts.
   - **Control charts for continuous data:**
     They comprise two graphs:
     - In the first the individual (I-chart) and / or mean values of the subgroups (Xbar-charts) are recorded. This first graph shows the variation between the subgroups in the Xbar charts.
     - The second graph depicts the changes of the values (MR-chart) and / or the ranges or the standard deviations of the subgroups and shows the variation within the subgroups (R / S-chart).
     The following equations are used for continuous data:

Calculating control charts manually

Type of control charts	Subgroup samples	Center line	Control limits	
Average and range	Constant and <10, but usually 3 to 5	$\overline{\overline{x}} = \dfrac{\left(\overline{x}_1 + \overline{x}_2 + \dots \overline{x}_k\right)}{k}$	$UCL_{\overline{x}} = \overline{\overline{x}} + A_2\overline{R}$	$LCL_{\overline{x}} = \overline{\overline{x}} - A_2\overline{R}$
Xbar-R		$\overline{R} = \dfrac{\left(R_1 + R_2 + \dots R_k\right)}{k}$	$UCL_R = D_4\overline{R}$	$LCL_R = D_3\overline{R}$
Average and range	Variable or ≥10	$\overline{\overline{x}} = \dfrac{\left(\overline{x}_1 + \overline{x}_2 + \dots \overline{x}_k\right)}{k}$	$UCL_{\overline{x}} = \overline{\overline{x}} + A_3\overline{s}$	$LCL_{\overline{x}} = \overline{\overline{x}} - A_3\overline{s}$
Xbar-S		$\overline{s} = \dfrac{\left(s_1 + s_2 + \dots s_k\right)}{k}$	$UCL_s = B_4\overline{s}$	$LCL_s = B_3\overline{s}$
Individual values and moving range	1	$\overline{x} = \dfrac{\left(x_1 + x_2 + \dots x_k\right)}{k}$	$UCL_x = \overline{x} + \dfrac{3}{d_2}\overline{R}_m$	$LCL_x = \overline{x} - \dfrac{3}{d_2}\overline{R}_m$
IMR		$\overline{R}_m = \dfrac{\left(R_1 + R_2 + \dots R_{k-1}\right)}{k-1}$	$UCL_{Rm} = D_4\overline{R}_m$	$LCL_{Rm} = D_3\overline{R}_m$
		$\overline{R}_m = \left|\left(x_{j+1} - x_j\right)\right|$		

(k is the number of subgroups)

Note on the IMR-chart: The constants (D_2, D_3 and D_4) for calculating the control limits are selected for n = 2 (number of observations used to calculate the moving range).

277

DEFINE

MEASURE

ANALYZE

IMPROVE

CONTROL

– **Control charts for discrete data:**

They comprise one graph and show the variation between the subgroups. The following equations are used for discrete data:

Calculating control charts manually

Type of control charts	Sample size	Center line	Control limits	
Proportion defective parts p-chart	Variable usually n > 5	$\bar{p} = \dfrac{\sum \hat{p}_i}{k}$ whereby $\hat{p}_i = \dfrac{\text{\# defective parts}}{n_i}$	$UCL_p = \bar{p} + 3\sqrt{\dfrac{\bar{p}(1-\bar{p})}{n_i}}$	$LCL_p = \bar{p} - 3\sqrt{\dfrac{\bar{p}(1-\bar{p})}{n_i}}$
Proportion defective parts np-chart	Constant usually n > 5	$\bar{p} = \dfrac{\sum \hat{p}_i}{k}$ whereby $\hat{p}_i = \dfrac{\text{\# defective parts}}{n}$	$UCL_{np} = n\bar{p} + 3\sqrt{n\bar{p}(1-\bar{p})}$	$LCL_{np} = n\bar{p} - 3\sqrt{n\bar{p}(1-\bar{p})}$
No. of defects per unit u-chart	Variable	$\bar{u} = \dfrac{\sum u_i}{k}$ where $u_i = \dfrac{\text{\# defects}}{n_i}$	$UCL_u = \bar{u} + 3\sqrt{\dfrac{\bar{u}}{n_i}}$	$LCL_u = \bar{u} - 3\sqrt{\dfrac{\bar{u}}{n_i}}$
No. of defects per unit c-chart	Constant	$\bar{c} = \dfrac{\text{\# defects}}{\text{\# units}}$	$UCL_c = \bar{c} + 3\sqrt{\bar{c}}$	$LCL_c = \bar{c} - 3\sqrt{\bar{c}}$

(k is the number of subgroups)

Note: the value zero limits the lower control levels (LCL) for discrete data. A negative value makes no sense.

Calculating control charts – manually/tables for the constants

Sample size n	Xbar-R-Chart			Xbar-S-Chart				Sample size n	IMR-Diagram		
	A_2	D_3	D_4	A_3	B_3	B_4	c_4		D_3	D_4	d_2
2	1.880	0	3.267	2.659	0	3.267	0.7979	2	0	3.267	1.128
3	1.023	0	2.575	1.954	0	2.568	0.8862	3	0	2.574	1.693
4	0.729	0	2.282	1.628	0	2.266	0.9213	4	0	2.282	2.059
5	0.577	0	2.115	1.427	0	2.089	0.9400	5	0	2.114	2.326
6	0.483	0	2.004	1.287	0.030	1.970	0.9515	6	0	2.004	2.534
7	0.419	0.076	1.924	1.182	0.118	1.882	0.9594	7	0.076	1.924	2.704
8	0.373	0.136	1.864	1.099	0.185	1.815	0.9650	8	0.136	1.864	2.847
9	0.337	0.184	1.816	1.032	0.239	1.761	0.9693	9	0.184	1.816	2.970
10	0.308	0.223	1.777	0.975	0.284	1.716	0.9727	10	0.223	1.777	3.078

Source: Montgomery, Douglas C. (2001), Introduction To Statistical Quality Control, 4th Edition, John Wiley & Sons

5. Draw up control charts

– The time interval to be examined is on the x-axis.

– The data points are recorded for each graph (analogous to a run chart).

– The center lines are then drawn and the control limits calculated and entered. The control limits are calculated using the before mentioned equations.

6. Interpret the control charts

– *Observe the center line*

Is the process centered in the correct position with respect to customer requirements or the target value? Was the process centered before? Has the process changed? Have customer requirements or the target value changed?

– *Analyze the data in relation to the control limits*

Are there common or special causes for the variation?

- The variance within the control limits is due to common causes in the process itself. They can only be reduced by introducing a change to the system or process.

- Data points outside or a pattern within the control limits (systematic deviations) indicate special causes. These need to be examined closely and eliminated before the control chart can be applied in process monitoring.

Is the process under control? A process is under control when all points lie within the control limits and no patterns are evident.

Computer programs like Minitab® test automatically if the process is under control. The other forms of testing are listed on the following page.

DEFINE

1	One point outside the control limits (3 Sigma from the center line)
2	9 consecutive points are on the same side of the center line
3	6 consecutive points, in ascending or descending order
4	14 consecutive points, alternating above and below the center line
5	2 of 3 consecutive points lie more than 3 Sigma from the center line (on the same side)
6	4 of 5 consecutive points lie more than 1 Sigma from the center line (on the same side)
7	15 consecutive points are located within the 1 Sigma limits
8	8 consecutive points lie more than 1 Sigma from the center line

MEASURE

ANALYZE

Example: generating a control chart (Xbar-R) for the paint workshop – manually

IMPROVE

	Week	Paint thickness	$\bar{x}$	R
February	1	167 / 155 / 184 / 154	165.00	30
	2	134 / 165 / 166 / 120	146.25	46
	3	188 / 174 / 157 / 166	171.25	31
	4	166 / 148 / 167 / 177	164.50	29
March	1	179 / 162 / 149 / 170	165.00	30
	2	178 / 182 / 140 / 123	155.75	59
	3	230 / 199 / 178 / 186	198.25	52
	4	175 / 158 / 181 / 192	176.50	34
April	1	193 / 168 / 159 / 150	167.50	43
	2	150 / 158 / 155 / 144	154.25	21
	3	187 / 181 / 172 / 169	177.25	18
	4	157 / 146 / 144 / 179	156.50	35

$$\bar{\bar{x}} = 166.50 \qquad \bar{R} = 35.67$$

CONTROL

DEFINE

MEASURE

ANALYZE

IMPROVE

CONTROL

Examples of Control Charts

Example: control limits for the control chart (Xbar-R) paint workshop – manually

Control limits for Xbar-chart	Control limits for R-chart

$UCL_x = \bar{\bar{x}} + A_2 \cdot \bar{R}$

$UCL_x = 166.50 + 0.729 \cdot 35.67 = 192.50$

$UCL_R = D_4 \cdot \bar{R}$

$UCL_R = 2.282 \cdot 35.67 = 81.40$

$LCL_x = \bar{\bar{x}} - A_2 \cdot \bar{R}$

$LCL_x = 166.50 - 0.729 \cdot 35.67 = 140.50$

$LCL_R = D_3 \cdot \bar{R}$

$LCL_R = 0 \cdot 35.67 = 0$

Example: control chart (Xbar-R) paint workshop – manually

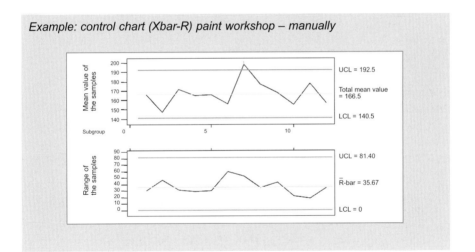

Further examples are given on the next page.

281

DEFINE

MEASURE

ANALYZE

IMPROVE

CONTROL

Example: control charts for continuous data, Xbar-R with Minitab®
The results show only common causes for variation. In addition, the values lie within the control limits.

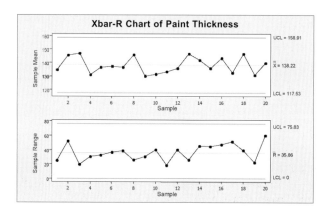

Example: for discrete data, p-chart with Minitab®
The results show no special causes.

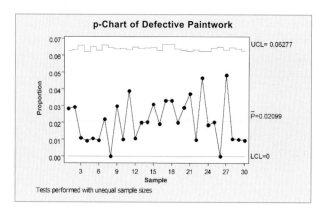

Reaction Plan

📁 **Term**
Reaction plan

🕐 **When**
Process monitoring, Control Phase

◎ **Goals**
– It is clear what is to be done when a CTQ is violated.
– Respond quickly and effectively to changes in a CTQ.
– Immediate reaction and launching of measures are possible.
– Control over what is happening.

Steps
1. Examine the improved process in detail for those places where a problem may occur, using an FMEA.
2. Derive the necessary measures for each point and nominate a responsible person.
3. Draw up a process management diagram.
4. Monitor the process. The reaction plan comes into force when a CTQ is violated or changes.

⇨ **Tip**
Take your time when drawing up a reaction plan – it is the Process Owner's most important document.

An example of a Process Management Diagram is given on the following page.

DEFINE MEASURE ANALYZE IMPROVE CONTROL

Example of Process Management Diagram

Process: Paintshop / accident repairs   *Process Owner:* F. Flintstone   *Date:* April 2006

Purpose: Control of paint quality in accident repairs   *Revision:* 17.5

Documentation					Monitoring				Reaction Plan	
Dept. A	*Dept. B*	*Dept. C*	*Dept. D*	*Dept. E*	*Output Measure-ments*	*Input-Process Measure-ments*	*Standard Specification*	*Method for Sampling Recording of Data*	*Immediate Solution*	*Process / System Improvement*
Order to repair					Under-stand-ability of the order		100 % of the employees with full un-derstanding	Weekly questioning of employees by measuring group		Monthly checking by customer ser-vice department head
	Repair of the body-work				Duration of the repair		Bodywork repair start at least 4 days before com-pletion date	Weekly sampling com-parison of completion date and repair com-pletion date by mea-suring group		Monthly checking by customer ser-vice department head
						Availability of spare parts	95 % avail-ability at the beginning of work	Full collection of data through IT, through person responsible for bodywork in stock	One person in stock is nomi-nated person responsible	
		Paint-ing			Paint thickness in micro-meters		Paint not more than 300 micro-meters after completion	Full collection of data through IT, through by dept. head at final control		Monthly checking by customer ser-vice department head
					Durability of paint		No rusting through paint within 5 years	Writing to the affected customers after 2, 4 and 5 years	Monthly letter action steered by IT according to date	Discussion of results in a monthly manage-ment meeting
					Proportion of internal rework		No more than 2 % in 90 days	Following monthly finance reports from the dept. head paint-work		Part of quality management reviews
					Depart-ment gross turnover			Following monthly finance reports from the dept. head paint-work		
						Availability of paint		Full collection of data through IT, through person responsible for bodywork in stock	One person in stock is nomi-nated person responsible	

Checklist for the Control Phase

Documentation

The new improved processes are documented in a complete and detailed way (in line with company guidelines). ☑

Detailed and understandable procedural instructions are drawn up. ☑

Monitoring

Key performance Indicators are selected and operationally defined. ☑

A data collection plan is drawn up and the capture of data is secured. ☑

The approaches for depicting and evaluating the data are defined. ☑

The Process Owners understand this depiction and evaluation. ☑

The Process Owners have agreed to undertake the monitoring. ☑

Reaction Plan

A reaction plan was developed. ☑

The Process Owners understand the reaction plan. ☑

The Process Owners have agreed to use the reaction plan. ☑

Implementation

Implementation is undertaken systematically until successful completion. ☑

Control

Carry out the Gate Review. ☑

DEFINE

MEASURE

ANALYZE

IMPROVE

CONTROL

Project Documentation

📁 **Term**
Project documentation

🕐 **When**
In the Control Phase

◎ **Goals**
- Communicate and place the working procedures at the disposal of other teams.
- Preserve the knowledge gained and the team know-how and utilize it as a best-practice benchmark in the company for further projects.
- Generate a basis for further improvements in the company.
- Secure the results and data for later comparisons.

▶▶ **Steps**
As a rule, project documentation consists of:
1. Project charter
2. Documentation of the individual project phases (project workbook, as a rule in MS PowerPoint®)
   - Phase goals
   - Tools used (which tool and why)
   - Phase results
3. Project tracking sheet
4. Implementation plan
5. Process management diagram (incl. should-be process flow)
6. Net-benefit sign off

⇨ **Tip**
It may make sense to add a summary of project work in the form of a management summary.

Example Project Workbook

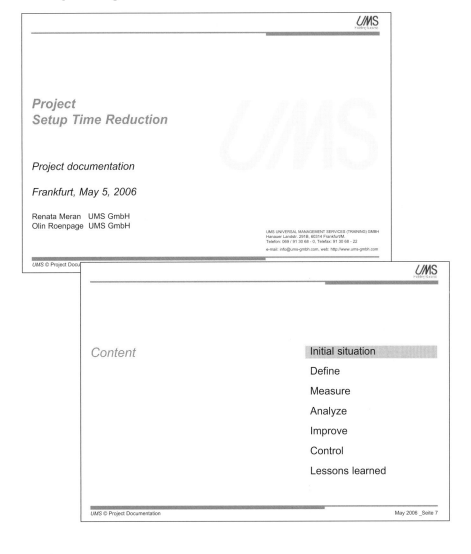

UMS

Project
Setup Time Reduction

Project documentation

Frankfurt, May 5, 2006

Renata Meran   UMS GmbH
Olin Roenpage   UMS GmbH

UMS UNIVERSAL MANAGEMENT SERVICES (TRAINING) GMBH
Hanauer Landstr. 291B, 60314 Frankfurt/M.
Telefon: 069 / 91 30 68 - 0, Telefax: 91 30 68 - 22
e-mail: info@ums-gmbh.com, web: http://www.ums-gmbh.com

UMS © Project Docu

UMS

Content

Initial situation
Define
Measure
Analyze
Improve
Control
Lessons learned

UMS © Project Documentation   May 2006 _Seite 7

Net Benefit Sign Off

The (expected) project benefit and the actual project costs (incl. implementation costs) are compared and the net benefit is calculated. As a rule, the net benefit sign-off is coordinated and agreed with the controlling department and signed by the project leader and the sponsor.

Project Closure

🗁 **Term**

Project closure.

When

When is the project closed?

– The project and improvement goals were achieved (compare with the project charter). To determine this, a statistical comparison should be carried out (before-after comparison) and the significant improvement can be proven using statistical tools.
– The employees have been actively involved in the implementation.
– The process is handed over to the owner.
– The whole project documentation is drawn up.

◎ **Goals**

– Official end: The project is handed over symbolically to the Process Owner.
– The Team Members are "discharged".

▸▸ **Steps**

– Call a final meeting with all those involved in the project and the Sponsor and Process Owner.
– The steps taken in the project and the most important insights and results are presented.
– The key experiences of the team are collected and documented in the sense of "lessons learned".

Tips

• Official recognition, a badge or a certificate are very important to the team.
• Evaluate the "mood barometer" accompanying the project to compliment the lessons learned.

Kaizen DMAIC

📁 **Terms**

Kaizen DMAIC, Six Sigma / DMAIC workshop

🕐 **When**

Either
- within the Analyze, Improve, or Control Phases, or
- alternatively to the usual DMAIC methodology

◎ **Goals**

- Shorten the DMAIC process for quick problem solution.
- Optimize already existing processes in both production and service sectors.

As distinct from the usual DMAIC methodology:
- Problem analysis and solution approaches are worked out in a workshop.
- The implementation of the measures decided on is carried out – if possible – within the workshop, otherwise immediately after its conclusion.

Prerequisite:
- The scope of the project is already identified, defined, and limited in the run-up to the workshop, e.g. long setup times, 5 S actions due to long search times in a clearly defined area, reduction of waste and prevention of defects on a production line.

▶▶ **Steps**

A Kaizen DMAIC is usually implemented in three phases:

1. Preparation

(Covers the Define and Measure Phases.)
- Define the problem in the Project / Workshop charter.
- Involve the team in an onboarding meeting and inform.
- Carry out the measurements.
- Collect information through research and interviews.
- Organize the workshop.

2. DMAIC Workshop
(Covers the Analyze and Improve Phases; max. 5 days.)
– Analyze the problem.
– Verify the causes of the problem with employees on site.
– Derive the solution approaches.
– Implement the solution approaches – if possible – within the workshop.

3. Post Treatment
(Covers the Improve and Control Phases; max. 2 weeks)
– Carry out the remaining measures, i.e. those not done in the workshop.
– Secure the sustainability, e.g. with new procedural instructions, visual process monitoring and regular trainings.

⇨ Tips
- Workshops usually demand a great deal of improvisation. An experienced project leader / facilitator and a detailed preparation help to realize the workshop as planned.
- Ensuring participation is crucial: the team members should always take part in the workshop, while management at least in part. This raises the appreciation of team work.
- Team membership can be reinforced symbolically (e.g. wearing the same shirts, caps, etc).
- The insights and knowledge gained should be discussed with those responsible at the end of the day.
- Because Kaizen DMAIC is a compressed DMAIC approach, use simple tools. Directly verify the cause hypotheses on site with quick samples together with the employees.
- With the project handover the Process Owner takes responsibility for ensuring that all measures still to be implemented are carried out.

Course of a Kaizen DMAIC workshop: Overview of the weeks

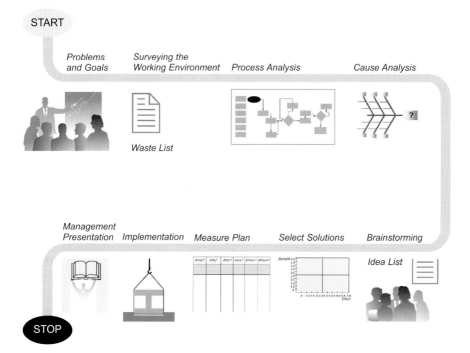

START

Problems
and Goals

Surveying the
Working Environment

Process Analysis

Cause Analysis

Waste List

?

Management
Presentation

Implementation

Measure Plan

Select Solutions

Brainstorming

Idea List

STOP

5S	Sort, Set in Order, Shine, Standardize, Sustain
ANOVA	Analysis of Variance
BB	Black Belt
Cap	Capacity
CCD	Central Composite Design
CEO	Chief Executive Officer
CIP	Continuous Improvement Process
CNX	Constant, Noise, Variable
CSI	Customer Satisfaction Index
CTB	Critical to Business
CTQ	Critical to Quality
DFSS	Design for Six Sigma
DMADV	Define, Measure, Analyze, Design, Verify
DMAIC	Define, Measure, Analyze, Improve, Control
DOE	Design of Experiments
DPMO	Defects per Million Opportunities
DPO	Defects per Opportunity
DPU	Defects per Unit
EVA	Economic Value Added
FMEA	Failure Mode and Effect Analysis
GB	Green Belt
h / hrs	Hour / hours
incl.	inclusive
ISO	International Organization for Standardization
IT	Information Technology
JIT	Just in Time
LCL	Lower Control Limit
LSL	Lower Specification Limit
Max.	Maximum
MBB	Master Black Belt

MGP	Multi Generation Plan
Min.	Minimum
min	Minute
Mm	Millimeter
MTBF	Mean Time Between Failure
MTTR	Mean Time to Repair
OEE	Overall Equipment Effectiveness
p. a.	per annum
PCI	Process Capability Index
PDCA	Plan, Do, Check, Act
PE	Process Efficiency
PFD	Process Function Diagram
PLT	Process Lead Time
PPM	Parts per Million
PC	Production Cycle
QFD	Quality Function Deployment
QM	Quality Management
R & D	Research and Development
R & R	Repeatability & Reproducibility
RPN	Risk Priority Number
RSM	Response Surface Method
RTP	Rolled Throughput
SCAMPER	Substitute, Combine, Adapt, Modify, Put to other uses, Eliminate, Reverse
SIPOC	Supplier, Input, Process, Output, Customer
SMART	Specific, Measurable, Agreed to, Realistic, Timebound
SMED	Single Minute Exchange of Die
SS	Safety Stock
StDev	Standard Deviation

SV	Study Variation
T.I.M.W.O.O.D	Transport, Inventory, Motion, Waiting, Overproduction, Overprocessing, Defects
TOC	Theory of Constraints
TP	Throughput
TPM	Total Productive Maintenance
TQM	Total Quality Management
UCL	Upper Control Limit
USL	Upper Specification Limit
VOB	Voice of Business
VOC	Voice of Customer
vs.	Versus
VSM	Value Stream Map
WIP	Work In Process

Yield	Process Sigma (ST)	Defects per 1,000,000	Defects per 100,000	Defects per 10,000	Defects per 1,000	Defects per 100
99,99966%	6,0	3,4	0,34	0,034	0,0034	0,00034
99,9995%	5,9	5	0,5	0,05	0,005	0,0005
99,9992%	5,8	8	0,8	0,08	0,008	0,0008
99,9990%	5,7	10	1	0,1	0,01	0,001
99,9980%	5,6	20	2	0,2	0,02	0,002
99,9970%	5,5	30	3	0,3	0,03	0,003
99,9960%	5,4	40	4	0,4	0,04	0,004
99,9930%	5,3	70	7	0,7	0,07	0,007
99,9900%	5,2	100	10	1,0	0,1	0,01
99,9850%	5,1	150	15	1,5	0,15	0,015
99,9770%	5,0	230	23	2,3	0,23	0,023
99,9670%	4,9	330	33	3,3	0,33	0,033
99,9520%	4,8	480	48	4,8	0,48	0,048
99,9320%	4,7	680	68	6,8	0,68	0,068
99,9040%	4,6	960	96	9,6	0,96	0,096
99,8650%	4,5	1.350	135	13,5	1,35	0,135
99,8140%	4,4	1.860	186	18,6	1,86	0,186
99,7450%	4,3	2.550	255	25,5	2,55	0,255
99,6540%	4,2	3.460	346	34,6	3,46	0,346
99,5340%	4,1	4.660	466	46,6	4,66	0,466
99,3790%	4,0	6.210	621	62,1	6,21	0,621
99,1810%	3,9	8.190	819	81,9	8,19	0,819
98,930%	3,8	10.700	1.070	107	10,7	1,07
98,610%	3,7	13.900	1.390	139	13,9	1,39
98,220%	3,6	17.800	1.780	178	17,8	1,78
97,730%	3,5	22.700	2.270	227	22,7	2,27
97,130%	3,4	28.700	2.870	287	28,7	2,87
96,410%	3,3	35.900	3.590	359	35,9	3,59
95,540%	3,2	44.600	4.460	446	44,6	4,46
94,520%	3,1	54.800	5.480	548	54,8	5,48
93,320%	3,0	66.800	6.680	668	66,8	6,68
91,920%	2,9	80.800	8.080	808	80,8	8,08
90,320%	2,8	96.800	9.680	968	96,8	9,68
88,50%	2,7	115.000	11.500	1.150	115	11,5
86,50%	2,6	135.000	13.500	1.350	135	13,5
84,20%	2,5	158.000	15.800	1.580	158	15,8
81,60%	2,4	184.000	18.400	1.840	184	18,4
78,80%	2,3	212.000	21.200	2.120	212	21,2
75,80%	2,2	242.000	24.200	2.420	242	24,2
72,60%	2,1	274.000	27.400	2.740	274	27,4
69,20%	2,0	308.000	30.800	3.080	308	30,8
65,60%	1,9	344.000	34.400	3.440	344	34,4
61,80%	1,8	382.000	38.200	3.820	382	38,2
58,00%	1,7	420.000	42.000	4.200	420	42
54,00%	1,6	460.000	46.000	4.600	460	46
50,00%	1,5	500.000	50.000	5.000	500	50
46,00%	1,4	540.000	54.000	5.400	540	54
43,00%	1,3	570.000	57.000	5.700	570	57
39,00%	1,2	610.000	61.000	6.100	610	61
35,00%	1,1	650.000	65.000	6.500	650	65
31,00%	1,0	690.000	69.000	6.900	690	69
28,00%	0,9	720.000	72.000	7.200	720	72
25,00%	0,8	750.000	75.000	7.500	750	75
22,00%	0,7	780.000	78.000	7.800	780	78
19,00%	0,6	810.000	81.000	8.100	810	81
16,00%	0,5	840.000	84.000	8.400	840	84
14,00%	0,4	860.000	86.000	8.600	860	86
12,00%	0,3	880.000	88.000	8.800	880	88
10,00%	0,2	900.000	90.000	9.000	900	90
8,00%	0,1	920.000	92.000	9.200	920	92

Note: Subtract 1.5 to obtain the "long-term Sigma".

Printing and Binding: Stürtz GmbH, Würzburg